WHEN JESUS SMILED

To laugh is to give oneself over to merriment.
To smile is to manifest a state of mind,
   either serene or melancholy, but without abandon.
One can smile with amusement
   or shaking one's head.
That would have been the case with Jesus,
   true God and true man
Living among men as he did,
Exactly like us.

Giorgio Conconi

When Jesus Smiled

Translated by Jordan Aumann, OP

ALBA·HOUSE   NEW·YORK

SOCIETY OF ST. PAUL, 2187 VICTORY BLVD., STATEN ISLAND, NEW YORK 10314

7956

ST PAULS

A translation from the Italian of *Quando Gesù Sorrise* by Giorgio Conconi, published by Edizioni San Paolo, Torino, 1995.

Quotations from the New Testament are taken from *The Alba House Gospels*, translated by Mark A. Wauck directly from the Greek and based on the third edition of the United Bible Society's *Greek New Testament* and the twenty-sixth edition of Nestle-Aland's *Novum Testamentum Graece*.

Library of Congress Cataloging-in-Publication Data

Conconi, Giorgio, 1937-
    [Quando Gesù sorrise. English]
    When Jesus smiled / Giorgio Conconi; translated by
Jordan Aumann.
        p.   cm.
    ISBN 0-8189-0768-1
    1. Jesus Christ — Humanity. 2. Jesus Christ — Humor.
3. Bible N.T. Gospels — Criticism, interpretation, etc.
I. Title.
BT218.C6613   1998
232.9 — dc21
                                    97-44733
                                    CIP

Produced and designed in the United States of America by the
Fathers and Brothers of the Society of St. Paul,
2187 Victory Boulevard, Staten Island, New York 10314,
as part of their communications apostolate.

ISBN: 0-8189-0768-1

Printing Information:

Current Printing - first digit   1   2   3   4   5   6   7   8   9   10

Year of Current Printing - first year shown

1998   1999   2000   2001   2002   2003   2004   2005

Table of Contents

Presentation

The Gospel is portrayed in living colors. We find there men like ourselves: impulsive and generous like Peter; avaricious like Judas; simple like the humble Publican or hypocritical and arrogant like the Pharisees (quibblers as well and treacherous); or else enamored and lost in a revery like Mary of Bethany, or a sinner, uneasy and alert, like the Samaritan woman at the well of living water.

There we also find the members of the animal kingdom: the donkey and the cow of the Christmas Crib; the sheep of the Good Shepherd; the innocent doves and the crafty serpent; the fox in its lair and the birds flying free in the air; the fish wriggling in the net and the pigs invaded by devils and jumping into the lake; the rooster who crows twice at the break of dawn. And there are trees, vines, olives and figs, the sycamore and the flowers — so many flowers! — and the grass in the meadow and the harvest in the fields. And then there are the little things of daily life: the water in the jug; the bread in the basket; the light under a bushel; the coin lost on the floor of the house; the stones that wound and kill; the oil that soothes the wounds; the wine that fortifies and gladdens the heart.

In spite of the fact that twenty centuries have passed, we feel at home in the pages of the Gospels, amid the scenes of everyday life. And then there are miracles, so numerous that they fill the eyes and the mind with amazement, but they are so much a part of the life of Christ among us that we get accustomed to them.

It is easy to picture Peter as an ordinary man who sometimes borders on the eccentric; it is also easy to picture the donkey on which the good Samaritan is riding; or the starving prodigal son who is tempted to take from the fodder that the pigs are eating; or to imagine Lazarus, still wrapped in the burial linens, arising and tottering to the entrance of the cave in which he had been buried. Even if painters had not vied with one another in the course of the centuries to portray these sacred events, we would still find in daily life — through personal experience or the example of others — images similar to those found in the pages of the Gospels. Indeed, they are a verification of the truth of the Gospels.

And what about Jesus, the principal actor in the Gospels? Art has given us impressive images of him and of every aspect of his life, images that are at once unpretentious and glorious, triumphant and sorrowful. But what was he really like? However much we try, we have no words or comparisons for probing the mystery of his glance, his countenance, his personality. We know that he was truly a man, and in this respect he was like us in all things. But we also know that he was God, and in this respect he transcends every category. We can draw close to his human dimension, but the divine totally escapes our sight. That is why the chief actor seems always to elude us (at least in part), as when he disappeared from the sight of his disciples. There is a part of his personality that will always remain in the shadow for us, although it is the luminous shadow of his divinity.

To try to discover what is concealed beyond the limits of this shadow is at least rash. Nevertheless, undaunted, Giorgio Conconi has tried to do so by restricting himself to one particular feature of the countenance of Jesus which manifests his hidden feelings: *when Jesus smiled....* But we know that a smile, like a word, is something more than a smile. Its real meaning is defined in terms of the context in which it occurs. Consequently, it can signify a wide variety of feelings, from condescension to compassion, from tenderness to whole-hearted sharing, from surprise and astonished amazement to a subtle expression of good humor, including good-natured — and yes! — smiling irony.... Giorgio Conconi has searched for that smile by extracting from the Gospels a series of passages in which this becomes the key to perceiving the feelings of Jesus and his benevolent reaction to the diverse and unpredictable actions of his contemporaries. First of all, he presents to the reader a particular incident as it is described in the Gospels; then he highlights those passages in which the smile of Jesus comes to the surface as an ineffable counter-point to the human event.

The author does not hesitate to use his imagi-nation in reconstructing the scene. He then gives his interpretation and commentary: "Jesus surely smiled, shaking his head"; "Once again, Jesus smiled"; "On hearing the mother's words, Jesus smiled."

This is a most unusual way of reading the Gospels (unusual in the sense that it is not very erudite or detailed or even rhetorical); it is a non-scholarly and somewhat "family-style" reading, but no less true for all that. On the contrary, it is even a more authentic reading, to the extent that the author is trying to portray the humanity of Jesus: his sharing with a smile in the weakness and suffering of man as well as the ingenuous but fervent response of his faith. This is what happens (we are at the last pages of the book) when Peter jumps into the water to more quickly join the Lord, who is waiting for him on the shore. The author describes the incident:

"Jesus is also happy. He smiles when he sees that the head of his Church suddenly realizes that he is naked and immediately wraps his outer garments around his waist. Peter then jumps into the water in order to be the first one to join him. Everyone in the boat is smiling. He who is on the shore also smiles when he sees that disciple with the beard swimming toward him as if he were trying to break a speed record, as if waving him a greeting with every powerful stroke."

Are not these pages a brilliant narrative which, superimposed on the dry, concise text of the Gospels, brings out certain implicit passages that are more human and humorous (from the outer garments to the beard, to the powerful swimming strokes, to the smiling applause of those who remained in the boat)? It is a reading that is modern, relevant and I dare say dynamic. It brings the mystery closer to us rather than making it more distant.

Yes, the part of Jesus that remains on the other side of the limits of the shadow is unattainable because it is his divine dimension. It resists every rash attempt to illuminate it and make it one's own. This is the threshold at which all literature stops in order to make room for faith, which must keep silent and adore. But that does not prevent literature — the written word and the imagination — from having its own authentic space that leads to faith and to piety. And in an age as sad as ours, even too erudite, sophisticated and terribly uncertain, we welcome a word that can introduce us to a smiling faith and a confident piety.

Giovanni Cristini

Introduction

For us Christians the Gospels have been proclaiming for almost two thousand years that the Son of God has come to earth but was accepted by very few; instead, he was rejected, insulted, scourged and killed. There could have been no worse reception on the part of his creatures.

But contrary to all human expectations, the earthly life of the Son of God could not come to a conclusion and in fact it did not end with his death, but with his resurrection and his glorious return to his heavenly Father.

No event in history could even remotely be compared with the history of Jesus. No one has ever been able to call himself man and God and then prove it, as he did. No one has ever died and risen again of his own accord. No one has ever died and risen by his own power.

If we examine the Gospels from this perspective, we must classify them as books of hope and joy. In spite of his tragic passion and death, Jesus was able to say: "I've conquered the world" (Jn 16:35). But his victory did not bring him or his faithful disciples any tangible reward. Nevertheless, it has projected a life without limits and beyond time for those who believe in him. Thanks to his teaching and his promise, we are destined for eternity.

True, our intellects are not able to comprehend all that, but that does not prevent us from accepting the many mysteries contained in his word and in his teaching. And our inability to understand should not surprise us too much. The human intellect cannot even explain fully the mystery of life to us who live it, nor the mystery of death to us who one day must die. The best we can do is accept life and death as phenomena that always accompany the days of our existence. Neither can anyone give an exhaustive explanation that will clarify the functioning of our body, our faithful servant for many decades, with its various organs, both large and small, noble and less noble; with their more or less complicated cell structure and with the variety of functions that are so perfectly integrated.

The limitations of our intellect are numerous, both as regards great things and small. But they are even more numerous when we consider the word of God. So we should not be surprised. This is a given fact.

We should not even be surprised if in reading and re-reading the Gospels, these books of a few pages that are an expression of the voice of God, we find a word or phrase which up to that time had escaped our notice or seemed to be of secondary importance, but actually contained a precious secret waiting to be revealed. The Gospels still preserve all the drama of the incidents narrated and they shake us Christians because of the hardness and blindness of our hearts. It is the same now as it was then.

God sends his Son to earth to save us from a fault that would condemn us, and although we are able to do so, we do not acknowledge him. Jesus lived with the apostles for a number of years; he frequently told them what would be the epilogue of his coming into the world, namely, his resurrection and his ascension into heaven. Nevertheless, even among the chosen ones there is one who has to put his finger into the wounds before he will believe.

Jesus manifested his infinite love to all, to generations past, present and future. And he showed his love even more to one, if that were possible. But that one will be the one who will deny him three times before the rooster crows twice.

Another one asks him the way to the Kingdom of Heaven and when he receives the information, he decides that it is impractical and too difficult.

Jesus' success here on earth constantly decreases; and he offers his last days to the honor and glory of God. To help us not to fall away, he reminds us of the brevity of life on earth compared to eternity. There will be sufferings and sacrifices for a brief time in exchange for an eternity of happiness.

But even if we review all the themes treated in the Gospels, all the events described, and all the revelations given to us, we shall never succeed in understanding these books of the Gospels unless we acknowledge their uniqueness. They are books of history, books about the word of God, books of drama, pedagogy, theology and poetry. They are all this and even more. Short books have sometimes been the occasion for thousands and thousands of pages written about them. So much so that common sense prompts us to ask: "What more could be written about the Gospels?"

Reading and re-reading the Gospels, we find that the word of God contained in them, addressed to man in the form of a narrative, does not overlook any of the characteristics of the human soul.

The Son of God was also endowed with a human soul, and there is one of his human attributes that has never been given its due: the smile of Jesus. How could he never have smiled during the days of his infancy and childhood? Or as an adult? Certainly there must have been many occasions for doing so — among his family members, among his disciples, and among those who followed him at a distance.

Jesus was an attentive observer of the characters and comportment of the people he met, of those who approached him or were beneficiaries of his miraculous power, of those who were close to him and were loved by him or loved him most. Being close to their pain and unhappiness, their evil deeds and cruelty, their blindness and stubbornness, he surely would have witnessed many examples of human folly which prompted him to smile, sometimes in amusement and sometimes shaking his head. This does not alter the fact that the men who were chosen by him or followed him, thanks to the grace of the Holy Spirit, later became saints. They are models of the Christian life for us and our guides on the road to salvation.

What we want to bring to your attention is the fact that frequently their foibles, great or small — and ours, too — can make us appear ridiculous without our wanting to do so. And if we admit this, we shall see that we are all equal: earthy, humble, seeking to be understood, in need of tolerance and of pardon.

On our part, we have selected various episodes to stimulate a greater desire to read the Gospels. They are the only books of all time and in the whole world that cannot be understood through and through; each time they are read, they reserve something for the next reading.

WHEN JESUS SMILED

The Chosen Ones

**Jesus selected his apostles one by one
from among the simple people.**

From the Gospel according to John (1:35-51):

The next day John was again standing there, as well as two of his disciples, and he looked right at Jesus as he was walking by and said, "Here is the Lamb of God." His two disciples heard him speaking and they followed Jesus.

Now when Jesus turned and saw them following him he said to them, "What are you looking for?" So they said to him, "Rabbi" — which, translated, means "Teacher" — "where are you staying?" "Come and see," he said to them. So they came and saw where he was staying, and they stayed with him that day; it was about four in the afternoon.

Now Andrew, the brother of Simon Peter, was one of the two who were listening to John and had followed him. He first found his own brother, Simon, and said to him, "We've found the Messiah!" — which, translated, is "Christ." He led him to Jesus. Jesus looked at him and said, "You are Simon son of John; you shall be called "Cephas" — which is translated, "Peter."

The next day he decided to go to Galilee, and he found Philip. And Jesus said to him, "Follow me!" Now Philip was from Bethsaida, from Andrew's and Peter's city. Philip found Nathanael and said to him, "We've found the one Moses wrote about in the Torah, as well as the Prophets — Jesus son of Joseph from Nazareth." And Nathanael said to him, "What good can come from Nazareth?" Philip said to him, "Come and see."

Jesus saw Nathanael coming towards him and said about him, "Here's a true Israelite, in whom there's no guile!" Nathanael said to him, "Where do you know me from?" Jesus answered and said to him, "Before Philip called you, while you were under the fig tree, I saw you." Nathanael answered him, "Rabbi, you're the Son of God, you're the king of Israel!" Jesus answered and said to him, "Do you believe because I told you I saw you beneath the fig tree? You'll see greater things than this!" And he said to him, "Amen, amen, I say to you, you'll see Heaven opened up and the angels of God ascending and descending upon the Son of Man!"

Jesus is presented by John the Baptist with an expression from the Old Testament: "Behold the Lamb of God!" (cf. Lv 4:32-35; Is 53:4-12). Under the Old Covenant God accepted the death of an animal as a substitute for the sinner condemned to death for his sins. In fact, sin carried with it a death sentence, insofar as the sinner is separated from

God. But with Jesus there is a change: he offers his life as a sacrificial lamb in order to take away the sins of men throughout the ages.

On a sunny day in the mild climate of Palestine people gather together on the shore of the river Jordan. The flowering bushes emit the perfume of springtime. John is baptizing and announcing the coming of the Son of God. Two of his disciples, having listened to the words inspired by the passing of Jesus, followed him immediately. Not needing an introduction, but knowing everything that lies in the heart of every man (Jn 2:25), Jesus looks back and sees that they are following him. He smiles. Then he asks them: "What are you looking for?" And the two respond somewhat awkwardly: "Master, where are you staying?"

We can imagine the mind of Jesus at that moment. Of all the answers he might have expected, this one is really funny. He smiles. "Come and see for yourselves." The abode of Jesus could not have been very large; nevertheless they stay with him. They are Andrew, the brother of Simon Peter, and John of Zebedee, the evangelist. They are both fishermen, possibly reasonably well off and perhaps members of a fisherman's cooperative, like Simon Peter and James, the brother of John.

Although Matthew describes the calling of the twelve apostles in a slightly different way, less detailed (Mt 4:18-22), the first attraction and the certitude that followed after they had met the Messiah are highly emphasized by all the evangelists. Andrew immediately finds his older brother Simon, who has a family, and tells him about meeting the Messiah. Simon looks at him in amazement and the two brothers communicate with each other in a glance. Andrew takes Simon in hand and leads him to Jesus. Jesus looks into his soul and changes his name. In the Bible that means to take possession of a person; it is like giving a man or woman a direction in life that is totally different from the one followed previously. It is the first time that the name "Cephas" (Peter) is used. It is an unknown name, and in Arabic it means rock, stone, a man of stone, solid.

The following day Jesus meets Philip of Bethsaida and he enlists him as one of the twelve. Twelve apostles, like the twelve sons of Jacob who gave their names to the twelve tribes of Israel. Philip leaves everything and follows Jesus without hesitation.

Some time later Philip meets the learned man Nathanael on the street and enthusiastically tells him what has happened: he has just met the one of whom Moses and the Prophets spoke — Jesus of Nazareth. "Well, imagine that!" says Nathanael indifferently. He is not the type to get excited. He then remarks to Philip that nothing good can come from Nazareth. It is a regional prejudice. The same thing is prevalent in the world today. Jesus surely smiles at this, shaking his head.

Philip doesn't mince words. "Come and see for

yourself." When Jesus sees the two approaching, he uses expressions that leave no room for doubt. First of all, he pays his respects to Nathanael, "an Israelite in whom there is no guile." Astonished, Nathanael asks: "How do you know me?" Jesus tells him that before Philip called him, he had already seen him meditating on the Scriptures under the fig tree, in accordance with the Hebrew custom. He was meditating on Jacob's dream (cf. Gn 28:12).

Nathanael is now deeply moved and he professes his faith in Jesus, the Son of God and the king of Israel. Then Jesus concludes: "Because I told you that I saw you under the fig tree, that was enough for you to believe. You'll see greater things than this." Jesus surely smiled as he said this.

Nathanael becomes the apostle with the name Bartholomew.

Next, he calls Matthew, son of Alphaeus. He is seated at a table in the shade of a huge tree, collecting taxes. He is rather severe. He likes money and the power it brings. He enjoys watching the faces of the people as they pay their money. Jesus passes by; he does not stop. And yet, all at once Matthew feels a surge of happiness. What a delightful experience to receive the attention of the Son of God! The happiness is so great that Matthew is impelled to share it by giving a huge banquet. Farewell to taxes and money! He becomes an apostle and an evangelist (Mt 9:9; 10:3; Mk 2:14; 3:15; Lk 5:27; 6:15).

In the following days, Jesus calls Thomas, James of Alphaeus and Thaddaeus, Simon the Canaanite and Judas Iscariot the traitor. No leader in the world has ever selected his subordinates in this manner nor from that class of people. Only Jesus. And when others objected, he answered with a smile. It is not difficult to join him.

The Wine at Cana

During a wedding reception at Cana the wine runs out.
Mary approaches Jesus and asks him to take care
of the situation. He does not want to intervene, and
Mary does not insist. She simply tells the
servants to do whatever Jesus wants.

From the Gospel according to John (2:1-12):

On the third day there was a wedding in Cana
of Galilee, and Jesus' mother was there. Now
Jesus was also invited to the wedding as well as
his disciples, and when the wine ran out Jesus'
mother said to him, "They have no wine." Jesus
replied to her, "What do you want from me,
woman? My hour hasn't come yet." His mother
said to the servants, "Do whatever he tells you."
Now six stone water jars were standing there, in
accordance with the Jewish purification rites,
each holding twenty or thirty gallons. Jesus said
to them, "Fill the water jars with water." And they
filled them to the brim. Then he said to them,
"Now draw some out and take it to the head
steward." So they took it. Now when the head
steward tasted the water which had become wine
— and he didn't know where it came from, while
the servants who had drawn the water did know

— the head steward called the bridegroom and said to him,"Every man first puts out the good wine, then when they're drunk [he puts out] the lesser wine; you've kept the good wine till now!" Jesus did this, the first of his signs, at Cana in Galilee and revealed his glory, and his disciples believed in him.

After this he, as well as his mother and brothers and his disciples, went down to Capernaum and stayed there for a few days.

John, the beloved disciple, the one who lived the longest, and the one who had the privilege of caring for the Virgin Mary until the end of her earthly pilgrimage, is the only one who records this incident, and he does so in his usual laconic way.

The life of Jesus before his public activity is unknown except for a few brief references: his presentation in the Temple, forty days after his birth; at the age of twelve, when he entered upon adulthood in the religious sense (Lk 2:22-40, 41-47). It is also recorded that "the child grew and became strong, and was filled with wisdom, and the grace of God was on him... [and he] progressed in wisdom and age and grace before God and men" (Lk 2:40, 52).

Until the age of thirty, he apparently grew up as an ordinary man, a model son, at first helping his father Joseph in the carpenter shop and then becoming a carpenter himself. Undoubtedly during all those years he would have had thousands of reasons for smiling as he observed the men and women he had come to save and who, we may rightly suppose, even created comical situations with or without intending to do so.

On that day at Cana, which is northeast of Nazareth, the weather is good; it is dry and cool. The sky is a deep blue. The wedding reception is a joyous occasion; the guests are numerous, even more numerous than those portrayed in the famous painting by Paul Veronese in the Louvre. Seated at long tables, the guests talk in loud voices to the groups near them. Every now and then a burst of laughter breaks forth and quickly spreads through the crowd.

Mary and Jesus have been invited, together with their relatives and the disciples of Jesus. Apparently Joseph is absent; perhaps because he is occupied elsewhere or because he doesn't care for parties, as is true of a grandfather or a father who is austere. But the absence is accepted without comment.

More and more time passes and more and more the party becomes joyful and merry. At a certain moment the wine runs out. Jesus is well aware of it, but Mary brings it to his attention: "They have no wine." Jesus look at her with surprise: "Why are you telling me? How can I do anything about it?" Perhaps in his heart he was already smiling, knowing what his mother would do in a few minutes.

As a matter of fact, Mary, knowing that she had an extraordinary son who could do everything and anything, whether big or small, acts like any other mother. She pays no attention to her son's refusal, but tells the servants to have recourse to him in order to solve the problem that could have ruined the wedding reception. She knows that Jesus cannot refuse if she asks him.

Mothers!

Jesus smiles, this time openly. He tells the servants to fill the jars to the brim with water. Then he asks them to draw some off and take it to the head waiter. With an air of self-importance that brings another smile to Jesus' face, the steward tastes the water-made-wine that will be famous throughout the centuries.

Jesus also smiles when he observes how all the guests appreciate and enjoy the results of his first and, for him, small miracle. John continues the narration by stating that the head waiter, satisfied with the quality of the wine, is profuse in his praise of the bridegroom for his generosity and his refinement. As always, to each his own.

The Long Wait Rewarded

A sick man, thirty-eight years old, is waiting at
the edge of the pool of Bethzatha to enter the water and
be cured. But that is granted only to the first one to be
immersed in the pool. Because of his illness,
the man always loses out to someone who can move more
quickly. Up to this time the man has not left the edge of
the pool. But he has faith that sooner or later he will
receive the miraculous cure. Jesus rewards him.

From the Gospel according to John (5:1-9):

After these things there was a festival of the
Jews, and Jesus went up to Jerusalem. Now in
Jerusalem by the Sheep Gate is a pool — called
Bethzatha in Hebrew — which has five porticoes.
In these would lie a crowd of sick people —
blind, lame, paralyzed. Now a man was there
who'd been sick for thirty-eight years. When
Jesus saw him lying there and learned that he'd
already been there a long time he said to him,
"Do you want to be healthy?" The sick man answered him, "Lord, I have no man to put me into
the pool when the water's been troubled, so
when I come, another goes down before me."
Jesus said to him, "Get up, pick up your cot and
walk." And at once the man became healthy and
picked up his cot and walked.

According[1] to the archaeological diggings, the pool was located northwest of the fortification of Santa Anna, north of the esplanade of the Temple. The installation consisted of two pools dug out of the rock and divided by a wall twenty-four and a half feet (seven and a half meters) long. The size of the pools was 157.5 and 223 square feet (48 and 68 square meters) respectively. Along the four walls there were four porticoes; the fifth one was above the dividing wall. It is not known for certain what caused the periodic movement of the waters of the pool. Historians are inclined to accept the theory that it is caused either by a flow of water that has collected in a basin at a higher level or by occasional gusts of wind. As to the possibility of the intervention of an angel, they leave that to popular belief. That makes one smile because to be objective and credible in the eyes of the world, prudence dictates that one should not believe in the direct action of spiritual beings, unless perhaps their help in times of danger, difficulty or at the moment of death. This would be acceptable even to those who like to call themselves non-believers.

So there are always persons suffering from various kinds of illness who are waiting around the pool of Bethzatha in the hope of a miraculous cure. Some of them are wailing in a loud voice; others wait in silence for the favorable moment. If in our day, in spite of the great progress in the medical sciences,

---

[1] A. Wilkenhauser, *Das Evangelium nach Johannes*.

one still speaks of incurable diseases, we can imagine what the situation was like in those times. It was very difficult to make a diagnosis when they could not possibly know the cause and consequently were unable to effect a cure.

Gathered around the pool are sad cases of very serious illnesses. And there is no distinction between the young and the old, the rich and the poor. The man who has been sick for thirty-eight years, and perhaps partially paralyzed, is among those who are waiting for a cure. We do not know how long he has been waiting, but it is certainly a long time. He knows that his cure is only a few steps away. All he has to do is be the first one in the pool when the waters are agitated (and we like to think that the water is moved by an angel). But for that paralyzed man a few steps are not a simple matter nor easy to accomplish. For him it is a distance impossible to traverse. When it is a question of one's health, there is no respect of persons. Much less for one's place in line.

As soon as the waters move and thus have the power of healing, there is always someone who is faster and gets into the pool first. Someone else may be carried to the edge of the pool in time but he does not notice the first movement of the water. In that moment there ensues a contest that is at the same time dramatic and grotesque. The strength of the competitors is quickly exhausted. The fastest and the most clever emerge victorious. As for the others, they must manage as well as they can.

So our poor paralytic waits. He does not despair, he does not give up, he does not leave. He has gone on like this for years. Maybe that is why he arouses the sympathy of Jesus. The Master passes through the sick in silence. He shares in their suffering. He walks slowly. The expression on his face, the bearing of his shoulders, of his arms — every movement reveals a humanity without any imperfection.

At a certain point he stops in front of the meek and patient paralytic. He speaks to him with utter simplicity, asking him if he wants to be cured. This was simply to get to the heart of the matter, and not to get an answer which is already implied in the very fact that the man is at the edge of the pool. As if Jesus did not already know, the sick man explains his difficulty in moving and hence his inability to be the first one in the pool. For that reason he has not yet been cured. He speaks in simple words and without any rancor against the persons who may have trampled on him or blocked his passage to the pool. This causes Jesus to smile with affection. The meek always move him. They are the ones who receive the full generosity of his love. The sick man, persevering and confident, has been waiting for years to be cured by some supernatural power. His request is definitively granted by the will of Jesus in person, the living God. All he has to do now is to pick up his cot and walk away on his own legs.

For him, a cure; for us, a lesson in perseverance.

No One is Believed
in His Own Country

Jesus returns to Nazareth and his fellow-countrymen seem to be more interested in concentrating on his humble origin and on his no less humble relatives than on his teaching and miraculous deeds.

From the Gospel according to Mark (6:1-6):

Jesus left there and came to his hometown, and his disciples followed him. When the Sabbath came he began to teach in the synagogue, and many of those who were listening were amazed and said, "Where did this fellow get all this? What's the wisdom given this man that such mighty works should come about at his hands? Isn't this the carpenter, the son of Mary and the brother of James and Joses and Judas and Simon? Aren't his sisters right here among us?"[2] And they rejected him. Jesus said to them, "A prophet is without honor only in his hometown and among his kinsmen and in his own house." He was unable to do any mighty works there, except that

---

[2] In Semitic usage any close relative can be referred to as brother or sister, as is done today in some parts of the world where a member of the same tribe or village is called brother or sister.

he cured a few sick people by laying his hands
on them, and he was astounded at their unbelief.

Jesus, born at Bethlehem, grew up and spent
the greater part of his life in Nazareth. That is why
he was often called "the Nazarene." Therefore, he
did not return later to Nazareth as a stranger. In fact,
he was well known and was actually famous. But he
knows from the outset that he will not be received
with any fanfare. Nevertheless, he does not want to
deprive his adopted town of the precious gift of his
visit.

Nazareth is a bit like the Christian world today: Jesus is certainly well known, but not always
thought of as the Son of God.

So Jesus returns to Nazareth with his disciples.
His fame has preceded him but it has left his fellow-
countrymen indifferent. Jealousy can make even the
sharpest eyes dull. When the Master walks through
the streets with his disciples, very few people come
out of their houses to greet him. Most of them are
content to peer out of the windows without being
seen. Jesus would certainly be amused at such con-
duct. The heads suddenly disappear into the shad-
ows when his glance falls in their direction!

On the Saturday after his arrival he goes to the
synagogue. Seated in the midst of his friends, he
begins to instruct them. Many of the people present
for the religious services approach the small group

and begin to listen to Jesus. Immediately they are astonished at what they hear, but very soon they become angry. They do not accept his authority.

"Who is this fellow?" "Who does he think he is?" "From which teacher did he get all that he is saying?" Such are the questions raised on all sides. Then, almost in unison: "We know very well that he is a carpenter from our town. We also know his family: his mother Mary, his cousins James, Joses, Jude and Simon,[3] and his other relatives. They are all common people who don't even believe in him."

His fellow-citizens make it clear that they would heed his words only if Jesus could prove that he is the disciple of some famous doctor of the law or at least that he is of noble birth. Not only is Jesus not accepted, but they see him as a scandal. Jesus smiles, this time shaking his head.

And how does he respond to the behavior of the citizens of Nazareth? With an act of kindness. He leaves the synagogue with his companions, turning his back on the angry voices that continue talking even when they can no longer be heard. But one person, a sick man burdened with troubles and without hope, pays no attention to what the people say. Avoiding the gaze of the crowd, he follows after Jesus and returns home cured. Jesus knows that it is not always through faith that people approach him,

---

[3] James became head of the church at Jerusalem; Jude is generally considered the author of an epistle.

but he accepts that fact also, smiling perhaps.

And it's good that he does so now. Later on, when he casts the money-changers out of the Temple, he won't be smiling.

The Opinion of Others

When everybody is beginning to talk about Jesus because of his teaching and his miracles, many people, including Herod, are expressing their opinions about his identity.

The Gospel according to Mark (6:14-16):

> King Herod heard [about Jesus], for his name had become known, and he said, "John the Baptizer has been raised from the dead, and that's why these powers are at work in him." But others said, "He's Elijah," while others said, "He's a prophet like one of the Prophets." But when Herod heard, he said, "John whom I beheaded, he's been raised!"

By that time the Messiah had been awaited for many years. The Jewish people were very conscious of the fact and they knew that the Messiah could come at any moment.

Now Jesus comes, preaching the word of God and performing miracles that God alone can do. He is renowned throughout Palestine. But not because he is recognized as the Messiah, the Son of God. For the majority of people his fame rests on his message of wisdom and hope, on the sick who are cured and the resurrection of some people from the dead. The people don't want to have anything to do with God. They don't want to give an account of their actions to anyone. Much less to him who cannot be vanquished by cunning or by reticence.

But by this time in Palestine it is not possible to ignore the presence of Jesus and everyone is asking who he could be. Everyone wants to know. It has always been so, and it is so today and will be in centuries to come. "Who is Jesus?" they asked then. "Who is Jesus?" people will be asking until the end of time.

"He is Elijah," says one; "He is a prophet like one of the Prophets," say others. Or again: "John the Baptizer has risen from the dead and that is why he has the power to work miracles."

Yes, Herod also wanted to know. He asks those around him to tell him. He wants first-hand information and indisputable proof. He had beheaded John the Baptizer and now his mind is confused and uncertain. This Jesus prevents him from sleeping at night. There must be some connection between him and John the Baptizer. Herod paces through the halls and salons of his sumptuous palace. Of every dignitary he asks: "Who is this Jesus?" But none of the answers are convincing. Finally he concludes on his own initiative: "That John the Baptizer whom I beheaded, he's been raised!"

To have a holy and just man like John the Baptizer beheaded was not difficult for Herod, but now,

faced with his ghost, it is terrifying. And Herod realizes that you can't behead a ghost!

Jesus smiles. And we presume that he smiles
also today at the answers given by many to the question: "Who is Jesus?"

Who Touched My Cloak?

Hemmed in by the crowd, Jesus is reprimanded by his
disciples when he asks who touched his cloak.

Notice the critical statement of Mark about doctors.
Luke, who was a physician, says simply that
no one could cure the affliction.

The Gospel according to Mark (5:24-34):

A large throng was following [Jesus] and kept
crowding in on him. Now a woman was there
who had had a heavy flow of blood for twelve
years and had suffered greatly at the hands of
many doctors. She'd spent all she had but had
gained nothing; on the contrary, it kept getting
worse. Having heard about Jesus, she came with
the crowd and touched his cloak from behind,
because she said, "If I can just touch even part of
his cloak I'll be saved." At once her flow of blood
dried up, and she knew in her body that she was
cured from the illness. Jesus himself realized at
once that power had gone out from him and he
turned around in the crowd saying, "Who
touched my cloak?" His disciples said to him,
"You see the crowd pressing in on you! How can
you say, 'Who touched me'?" But he kept look-

ing around to see who had done it. Then the woman, trembling and afraid because she knew what had happened to her, came and fell down before him and told him the whole truth. But he said to her, "Daughter, your faith has saved you; go in peace and be cured of your illness."

From the Gospel according to Luke (8:42-48):

Now as he was going the crowd kept pressing in on him. A woman was there who had had a heavy flow of blood for twelve years that couldn't be cured by anyone. She came up and touched the hem of his cloak from behind, and immediately the flow of blood stopped. And Jesus said, "Who was it that touched me?" When everyone denied it Peter said, "Master, the crowd is pressing in on you and crowding around!" But Jesus said, "Someone touched me — I could feel power going out from me." When the woman saw that she couldn't hide she came, trembling, and fell down before him and, in the presence of all the people, she told why she'd touched him and how she'd been immediately cured. So he said to her, "Daughter, your faith has saved you; go in peace!"

Matthew also refers to this episode of the hemorrhaging woman (Mt 9:20-22) but in only a few lines, as if it were only one of many miracles. He places more emphasis on faith as the cause of the cure than on the cure which was the consequence of faith. We must say that, of the three accounts, the only person who could have been an eyewitness is Matthew. It must have been a cure that caused a good deal of attention. Mark could have had the report of the cure from Peter; Luke took it from the text of Mark.

Jesus' fame travels through Palestine faster than the desert wind. He continues to increase the number of his disciples who acknowledge him to be the Son of God. Large crowds press around him, seeking some kind of a cure or a teaching that will increase their hope. It is not the usual sight in the streets and squares of that country.

Moreover, it is difficult to get close to Jesus. No one wants to make room for others. The closer one can get to him, the better it is. One woman who has been sick for many years tries to get through the wall of people that separates her from the Master. She has to worm her way through the group standing around him, advancing a step at a time. The enthusiasm and confusion make it easier for her to get through. Finally she is standing behind him. She trembles. She doesn't dare. Then she hesitates no longer. It's now or never. Either him or no one.

After the woman's cure, Jesus asks: "Who touched my cloak?" Someone standing close to him responds in the negative. He doesn't understand what Jesus means. Therefore it is excellent foresight to exonerate oneself with a "I had nothing to do with it." One never knows.

The disciples (according to Mark) or Peter himself (according to Luke) quickly respond to Jesus' question. They do so with a certain sense of self-confidence and in words that portray Jesus as being very ingenuous.

"What! You can't even move because of the crowd that presses so closely that you can't breathe, and you ask who touched your cloak? Look around; there are so many people that you can't even count them! Someone may have touched you without intending to do so. So why this fuss? You should be used to this by now."

Jesus really has to smile at the simple-minded retort of his disciples. Paying no attention to their words and the mentality that gave rise to them, he lets his gaze wander over the people near him. He knows that it was someone behind him.

He waits for the woman who had touched the border of his mantle to make herself known. In a little while she kneels at his feet, fearful and trembling.

"It was I," she exclaims in front of all the people, "because I have been suffering for years and I had no more strength or hope. Now I am cured; I am no longer unclean.[4]

Jesus now makes the statement that astonishes

---

[4] According to the Jewish religion, the woman was suffering from an affliction that made her legally unclean. That would have prompted her to surreptitiously touch the cloak of Jesus rather than present herself with a request for a cure.

his disciples at that time and at all times thereafter: "Daughter, your faith has saved you." We tend to emphasize the fact that the miraculous healing took place without the explicit consent of Jesus. The truth of the matter is, as he says later, he was aware that power had gone out from him. This is very moving. Faith was sufficient. First the woman is granted her request; then she is questioned. There is a lesson here for us also.

But this incident contains another element that made Jesus smile: the way the evangelists speak of doctors. All three of them (Mark, Luke and Matthew) agree that the woman's sickness had lasted for a long time. Twelve years. Mark, however, differs from the others by criticizing the doctors of his time. In a few verses he delivers sharp jabs that even today annoy those who put all their faith in doctors. Was Peter the source of those verses? Perhaps.[5]

Mark says that the woman "had suffered greatly at the hands of many doctors" (5:25). She had gone from one doctor to another and had one consultation after another. The only result was that her suffering constantly increased. Not only that, but in addition to the physical suffering there was the financial loss. Doctors were expensive even in those days.

And what was the result? There was no im-

---

[5] It is said that Mark's written account of the life of Jesus came from the lips of Peter.

provement; rather, the woman's condition got worse and worse. Those few verses of the Gospel leave no means of escape for the doctors. There are not even any extenuating circumstances. And Luke, using the Gospel of Mark to redact his own, and being a doctor himself, must have jumped from his seat when he read Mark's sharp criticism of doctors. He has no doubt whatever about correcting and softening the narration for himself and for his colleagues. In fact he simply says that "a woman was there who had a heavy flow of blood for twelve years that couldn't be cured by anyone" (8:43).

We tend to agree more with Luke. If only Jesus, who is God, was able to cure the woman, that is proof that it was impossible for poor mortals to do so, even if they were doctors.

Looking from on high at the three versions of the episode as related in the Gospels, Jesus must certainly be smiling again.

The Pharisees Criticize Jesus

The Pharisees and their scribes criticize Jesus and his
disciples for sitting at table with Levi and the other
publicans. Silenced by a well-deserved rebuke,
they protest that the disciples of John
keep a fast, while those of Jesus eat and drink.

From the Gospel according to Mark (2:13-17):

Once again he went out along the sea, and
the whole crowd came to him and he taught
them. As he walked along he saw Levi son of
Alpheus seated at his tax booth, and he said to
him, "Follow me!" And he got up and followed
him. Now he reclined at table in Levi's house,
and many tax collectors and sinners were at table
with Jesus and his disciples; many, indeed, were
there. Also following him were scribes of the
Pharisees, and when they saw that he was eating with sinners and publicans, they said to his
disciples, "Why is he eating with tax collectors
and sinners?" When he heard this Jesus said to
them, "The healthy aren't in need of a doctor —
the sick are! I came to call sinners, not the righteous."

From the Gospel according to Luke (5:33-35):

Then they said to him, "John's disciples often fast and offer prayers, and likewise the disciples of the Pharisees, but yours eat and drink. So Jesus said to them,

> "Can you make the groomsmen fast
>   while the bridegroom is with them?
> But the days will come, and when the groom
>   is taken from them,
>   then they'll fast in those days."

Matthew, called from the tax collector's booth to change his life forever, wants to show his joy by arranging a banquet for everybody: his fellow tax collectors, his friends, and his new companions with their Master. Long tables are set up in the cool shade of the house. These are pleasant moments in the company of Jesus, who has snatched from their mundane tasks men who now, without really knowing why, feel very happy. To find and follow Jesus does call for sacrifice and renunciation, but it also brings peace and joy.

This seems to be a really good celebration and we would also like to join in. But now the habitual critics, the Pharisees and their scribes, have something to say. There are always some people who get a great deal of satisfaction in spoiling the fun.

The Pharisees and their scribes summon up their courage to ask the disciples about the behavior of Jesus. Their questions are already a condemnation: "Does it seem right to you that one who declares that he is the Messiah should choose such company? Look at them; we know them all very well. They are the scum of the earth: publicans and sinners. People who live by sucking the blood of their own countrymen."

Jesus hears this and smiles. He is used to criticism, however absurd. Here he is, the God-man, being criticized with absurd statements concerning his behavior. What must one say to make oneself understood by this world? But he also knows that the human intellect can reach limits undreamed of or unexpected by man himself. But it requires patience and perseverance. Such great perseverance. So much patience.

So Jesus responds to the provocation with a few words of great consolation for one who considers himself a sinner: "The healthy aren't in need of a doctor — the sick are! I came to call sinners, not the righteous."

Are the Pharisees satisfied? They would be, if there were not another problem. If Jesus is right, then why do the disciples of John fast but his disciples eat and drink?

Jesus shakes his head and smiles again. What blockheads! The Pharisees and their scribes do not understand that when the disciples are deprived of his physical presence, they will have time — all the time they want — to fast and suffer.

Jesus in the House of Jairus

**On one occasion, in the house of Jairus,
Jesus is laughed to scorn for saying that the daughter
of Jairus is not dead but sleeping.**

From the Gospel according to Luke (8:49-56):

Now when Jesus returned the crowd welcomed him, because they'd all been looking for him. And, behold, a man named Jairus came — he was a ruler of the synagogue — and he fell at Jesus' feet and begged him to come to his house, because he had an only daughter about twelve years old who was at the point of death.

* * *

While he was still speaking someone came from the ruler of the synagogue's and said, "Your daughter has died; don't trouble the teacher further." But Jesus heard this and told him, "Don't be afraid! Just believe and she'll be saved!" When he came to the house he didn't allow anyone to go in with him except Peter, John and James, and the mother and father of the child. Now everyone was weeping and mourning for her, but he said, "Don't weep — she hasn't died, she's sleeping!" And they laughed at him because they knew she had died. Then he grasped her hand and called out, "Child, arise!" Her spirit returned and she immediately sat up, and he gave instructions that she be given something to eat. Her parents were beside themselves, but he ordered them to tell no one what had happened.

This passage calls for some comments, both big and small. For example, it demonstrates the power of faith, which should not weaken, even in the face of that which reason sees as factual evidence. Here it has to do with death. The drama is finally over for a girl twelve years old and for her parents, of whom she is the only daughter.

Jesus is not in a hurry. He knows and even teaches what is contrary to the factual evidence. At that time relations between the great majority of priests, scribes, Pharisees and Jesus were not very good, nor, we imagine, between the ruler of a synagogue and Jesus. But now it is a question of the life of an only daughter. The Master has a confirmed reputation as a healer. All the others have failed; it is necessary to turn to him. It doesn't make any difference that according to Mark (5:21-24) and Luke the girl is at death's door or according to Matthew (9:18-19) she is already dead.

The ruler of the synagogue goes to Jesus. He doesn't give any thought to the problem of what those at the synagogue or the rest of the faithful will say. He doesn't take any precautions. Arriving in front of the Master, he throws himself at his feet.

He begs him. The sorrow of a father over the loss of a daughter or a son is among the greatest sorrows. Jesus knows that very well. But he waits. There is no need to hurry. It is already written how it is to turn out. He pauses awhile with the woman suffering from the flow of blood and cures her. Another miracle, a fruit of faith.

From the house of the ruler of the synagogue comes someone to announce that it's all over: the girl is dead. Jesus pays no attention to the news. He takes with him three disciples — Peter and the two Boanerges: James and John, the sons of thunder — and sets off for the house of Jairus.

There he finds the flute players and the mourners weeping and moaning. Jesus does not get upset but with great composure he quietly asks them to leave because, as he says, the girl is not dead but sleeping. The music stops and a heavy silence falls over the house. The people begin to leave, but suddenly someone recovers from the shock caused by Jesus' words and the reaction is contagious. The crowd of mourners gives vent to laughter, scorn and derision. "Who does he think he is?" "He thinks he knows everything, but this time he has made a serious mistake." "Watch out. He's going to teach us now when a person is dead or just sleeping."

Confronted with this nonsense, Jesus cannot help but smile sadly. Nevertheless, it is not pleasant to be ridiculed by such nasty people. He can anticipate what their reaction will be after he has laid hands on the girl. But he doesn't want a large number of witnesses; they don't deserve it. He wants only the mother and father and the three disciples to be with him. Only they will be able to see Jesus extend his hands over the corpse of the young girl and give the command: "Talitha, koum," which in Aramaic means "Little girl, I say to you, arise!" (Mk 5:41).

Immediately the girl is restored to life, gets up and begins to walk. The house seems filled with light. The air one breathes is now pure and invigorating. With great sensitivity Jesus tells them to give the girl something to eat. That is a sign that life has returned.

We can well imagine the joy of those present and also of Jesus, who loved children so much. The expressions on the faces of those who had mocked and derided Jesus cannot help but amuse Jesus, and us as well.

Jesus Awakes and Calms the Storm

A violent storm arises over the lake and the
waves are filling the boat with water. The disciples
are terrified, but Jesus is peacefully sleeping in the stern
of the boat. They wake him up with a reproach.

From the Gospel according to Mark (4:35-41):

That day when evening had come he said to
them, "Let's cross over to the other side." After
dismissing the crowd they took him as he was,
in the boat, and other boats were with it. A violent wind squall came up and the waves were
breaking over the boat so that by this time the
boat was filling up, yet he was in the stern, sleeping on the cushion. So they woke him and said
to him, "Teacher, doesn't it matter to you that
we're going to die?" Then he woke up and rebuked the wind and said to the sea, "Silence! Be
calm!" The wind ceased and there was a profound
calm, and he said to them, "Why are you afraid?
Do you still not have faith?" Then they were
seized with fear and said to each other, "Who is
he, then, that both the wind and sea obey him?"

This episode is also reported by Luke (Lk 8:22-

25) with other words that lend drama to the event: "Master, Master, we're going to die!"

Jesus gets into the boat just as he is; that is, without girding his cloak around his waist, not dressed in the usual manner for boating. It is almost evening and perhaps he is tired. He has preached to the disciples and the crowd for several hours. Now he asks to be transported to the other side of the lake. Other ships follow the one in which Jesus is riding. He goes to the stern of the boat, rests his head on a cushion and goes to sleep. His peaceful countenance is radiant as he yields to a restful sleep.

All of a sudden a strong wind arises, churning the waves to dangerous heights. The scent of the lake penetrates to the bones. The heavens descend low and become very dark. Almost all the disciples are fishermen but even those who are not, know well that one does not fool with the fury of Lake Tiberias. It may be calm at one moment and violently stormy in the next. One must immediately take the necessary precautions in order not to run into serious danger. The disciples know the signs and they realize that all of a sudden the storm could break. Very likely someone had said at the start that there is no need to worry because the Master is with them. By his words and his powers of healing he had already given an indication that he was more than a mere man.

But men have little faith when they are caught up in the fury of nature. Soon the boats find themselves in the grip of the storm. It is too late to try to maneuver out of danger. And Jesus is asleep in the stern as if the situation was no concern of his.

Panic spreads among the disciples like fire on dry wood. They cry out in terror. They awaken Jesus and without mincing words they shout at him: "Doesn't it matter to you that we are going to die?" And more than one calls out to him: "Master, Master, we're going to die!"

Jesus wakes up and perhaps he shakes his head, smiling, without paying much attention to the words of his disciples. We are back at square one, he thinks; their fear is greater than their faith.

He sees that there are other boats also in trouble. With a few words he calms the wind and the waves. Immediately all is tranquil.

But this does not suffice to calm the fears of his disciples. They don't utter a word of thanks to the one who saved them. They are now frightened by what happened. Jesus looks at them, smiling. What more can I do for these blessed men, he asks himself.

A little later, still in the boat, when the disciples have recovered from their terror, there remains only one question: "Who is he, then, that both the wind and the sea obey him?"

Jesus has good reason to ask where is their — and our — faith.

Peter Tries to Walk on the Water

Jesus walks on the water. Peter wants to imitate him,
but he tries to do so only up to a certain point.

From the Gospel according to Matthew (14:22-33):

At once he made his disciples get into the
boat and go on ahead of him to the other side
while he sent the crowds away, and after send-
ing the crowds away he went up the mountain
to pray in private. When evening came on he was
there alone, while the boat was already several
miles away from land, tossed about by the waves,
for the wind was against it.

Now shortly before dawn he came toward
them, walking on the sea. When the disciples
saw him walking on the sea they were terrified
and said, "It's a ghost!" and they cried out in fear.
But he spoke to them at once and said, "Take
courage! It's me! Don't be afraid!"

In answer to him Peter said, "Lord, if it's you,
command me to come to you on the water." So
he said, "Come!" Peter got out of the boat and
began to walk on the water and drew near to
Jesus, but when he saw the wind he became
frightened and, as he began to sink, he cried out
and said, "Save me, Lord!" At once Jesus reached

out his hand and caught him and said to him, "O you of little faith, why did you doubt?" And when they got into the boat the wind ceased. Then those in the boat worshipped him and said, "Truly, you're the Son of God!"

This incident is also reported by Mark (Mk 6:45-52) and by John (Jn 6:16-21), but perhaps Matthew, who was in the boat at the time, thought Peter's sinking in the water was humorous, so he handed it on to posterity. We know that when the leader is the subject of a comical incident it is all the more amusing to the rest.

These are the facts. Jesus commands his disciples to go before him in the boat to the other shore while he dismisses the crowd and goes up the mountain to pray. Perhaps he knows that they do not care very much for praying, especially if it takes a long time. Even at the end of his sojourn on earth, they fell asleep several times in the Garden of Gethsemane.

Meanwhile, the boat has covered several miles. The water is rough and there is a strong wind. Sometime between three and six in the morning Jesus decides to rejoin his disciples, walking on the water. The darkness is not yet totally dissipated by the dawn's early light. The Master approaches. When the disciples first see him they think it's a ghost and they are terrified at the sight. These strong, healthy men immediately cry out in fear. How would we have reacted in their place?

But these men have less of an excuse for acting as they did. They had been recruited some time ago and they had already witnessed numerous extraordinary events. And yet to be in a boat that is at the mercy of the waves and the violent wind, and at night to boot, one's courage could fail a bit. In addition, to see the Master walking on the water and coming toward them is not a usual occurrence. One could perhaps think that he has already passed on to the next world.

For his part, Jesus must be amused at seeing his disciples mistake him for a ghost and cry out in terror. Nevertheless, he does not want to leave them in this state of fear and anxiety. He is merciful even in little things. He doesn't want them to remain in the grip of fear, so he tries to calm them down immediately: "Don't be afraid; it's me, Jesus, in flesh and bone. Nothing will happen to you or to the boat."

And what response does he get? Peter calls out in return: "If it is really you, let me walk on the water too, and come to you." Jesus cannot help but smile at these words. "Come," he says.

Let's imagine Peter's state of mind: a bit fearful, a bit worried about taking on a project that everyone considers impossible, but also a bit happy at being able to show off in front of the other disciples. He climbs over the side of the boat and… "I'm walking!" he shouts.

He approaches Jesus. Suddenly he begins to doubt: "How is this possible? Am I awake or am I dreaming? No! This isn't possible! And in this strong wind?"

Jesus shakes his head and smiles again. Fear and doubt overcome Peter. Perhaps the disciples in the boat feel a certain satisfaction in seeing Peter falter.

"Master, save me!" he cries. Smiling, Jesus stretches out his hand and pulls him up out of the water. Then they both get into the boat and the lake becomes calm. The other disciples look on with great amazement. But there is one last smile: "Because of this small thing you acknowledge me as the Son of God!"

The Cry of the Blind Man

Bartimaeus, son of Timaeus, is seated on the
side of the road to Jericho, begging, when he learns that
Jesus is passing by. He starts calling out to him in hopes
of being cured. Those who are walking in front try to
silence him, but he only shouts all the louder.
Jesus hears him and cures him.

From the Gospel according to Luke (18-35-43):

Now it happened that when he was approaching Jericho a blind man was seated beside the road, begging. When he heard the crowds going by he asked what was going on and they told him, "Jesus of Nazareth is passing by." So he cried out and said, "Jesus, Son of David, have mercy on me!"

Those who were going ahead ordered him to be silent, but he kept crying out all the more, "Son of David, have mercy on me!" Jesus stopped and ordered the man to be brought to him, and when he approached he asked him, "What do you want me to do for you?" And he said, "Lord, that I might see again!" Jesus said to him, "Regain your sight! Your faith has saved you!" Immediately he could see again and followed Jesus, glorifying God. And all the people, when they saw this, gave praise to God.

This incident is also recorded by Matthew, but he speaks of two blind men (Mt 20:29-34), and by Mark, who gives us the name of the man and his father (Lk 10:46-52). Moreover, for these two evangelists the event took place as Jesus was leaving Jericho, not entering it. Mere details.

Let's recall the scene. The unhappy man is seated at the roadside, begging. He is wrapped in his cloak and in his darkness. Like all those who have lost their sight, he has sensitive ears. He can hear at a great distance. His vigil, which is usually in silence, is made more pleasant by the perfume of the earth, plants and flowers that is wafted from time to time on the warm, clean air. His thoughts are drawn to the remembrance of things that at one time he could see. But what is happening?

Dozens or even hundreds of voices are approaching. Jesus is always accompanied by a crowd. Bartimaeus, who is able to hear the solitary passage of an occasional pedestrian at a distance of many yards, now becomes very excited. He asks the first persons who approach him what is going on. When he learns that it is Jesus of Nazareth, the blind man immediately invokes the Son of David and asks to be cured.

The fact that Bartimaeus asks "that I might see again," indicates that he had become blind; he was not blind from birth. He knew what it was like to be able to see and he also knew what it meant to lose one's sight. Hence, this is a great and a unique opportunity that has come his way today: to be in the presence of the only one who can perform the miracle!

Bartimaeus shouts in order to make himself heard above the crowd. Those closest to him try to make him be quiet. His shouting is an annoyance to others and it shows a lack of decorum. Besides, the Master cannot take care of all the sicknesses in the world! So the blind man should remain quiet and peaceful.

Bartimaeus responds to this by shouting all the louder. The people are becoming impatient with him. And Jesus, who heard him from the outset, smiles at his insistence. He commands the disciples to bring Bartimaeus to him, and when they do, he asks the blind man what he wants. "Lord, that I might see again," is the immediate reply.

Once again, Jesus smiles. One does not ask that one's sight be restored from the first person he meets on the street. Rather, the blind man addresses his petition to one whom he calls the Son of David. In the face of such an act of faith, Jesus touches his eyes and the darkness that held Bartimaeus prisoner is dissolved. The light returns. We cannot even imagine the immense joy that Bartimaeus feels at that moment.

Judas Reprimands Mary of Bethany

Mary, the sister of Lazarus, is scolded by Judas
and perhaps by some of the other disciples for anointing
the feet of Jesus with oil of nard, instead of saving it in
order to sell it and give the proceeds to the poor.

From the Gospel according to John (12:1-11):

Six days before the Passover, Jesus came to
Bethany where Lazarus was, whom Jesus had
raised from the dead. They had a banquet for
him there and Martha served, while Lazarus was
one of those who were reclining at table with
him. So Mary took a pound of very expensive
pure oil of nard and anointed Jesus' feet and
wiped his feet dry with her hair; and the house
was filled with the fragrance of the oil.

Then Judas Iscariot, one of his disciples, the
one who was going to hand him over, said, "Why
wasn't this oil sold for three hundred denarii and
given to the poor?" Now he said this not because
he was concerned about the poor but because he
was a thief; and since he kept the money bag he
used to take what was put in it. So Jesus said, "Let
her be; let her keep it for the day of my burial,
for

The poor you always have with you
But me you do not always have."

So a large crowd of the Jews found out that
he was there and they came, not just because of
Jesus, but also to see Lazarus, whom he'd raised
from the dead. Now the chief priests were plot-
ting to kill Lazarus, too, because many of the
Jews were leaving on account of him and were
coming to believe in Jesus.

This incident from the life of Jesus is presented
as a joyful time in the company of his friends in
Bethany: Martha, Mary and Lazarus, who was recently raised from the dead and is therefore amazed
at being back in the world.

It is only two days before the Jewish Passover,
which commemorates the liberation of the Jews
from Egypt. The disciples are with the Master at the
banquet, and Martha, as usual, is most diligent in
waiting on the guests. She is continually going back
and forth, carrying serving plates and jugs of wine,
responding to their every request. It is not necessary to ask; she usually knows their needs intuitively,
even before they speak or cast a glance in her direction. The house is cool, but with all that she has
to do, she feels very warm. But she bears it all without complaint.

Mary, on the other hand, excited and joyful
at the presence of the Master, stays close to him in
order to gaze on him and listen to his words. At a

certain moment her happiness prompts her to pick up an alabaster vase containing a perfumed oil. She anoints the feet of Jesus and dries them with her hair. The house is permeated with the aromatic perfume of nard. This must be very pleasing to everyone.

But someone has to protest. It is Judas Iscariot, and with him, as it is written in the Synoptics, one of the other disciples. There have always been those who make themselves judges over others, and even over the Master himself. It is a type of behavior that makes one smile.

Judas asserts absolutely that the perfume is worth three hundred denarii.[6] Therefore that amount of money has been taken from the poor. And since Jesus did not tell Mary to stop, he is included in the reprimand of Judas.

Jesus has to smile at this severe scolding from some of his disciples. Anyone who criticizes what Mary is doing does not understand either the immediate significance of her action or the deeper meaning that is related to the passion and death of Jesus. There will be thousands and thousands of opportunities to help the poor, and in the centuries to come the number will be infinite. But there is not much more time to honor the Master, because his hour is very close.

John, who is a witness to the anointing of the feet and the subsequent scolding, immediately puts

---

[6] In those days one denarius was equivalent to a day's wages.

Judas in his place by accusing him of being an accomplished thief and denying that he is at all concerned about the poor. He is far from being altruistic! He holds the common purse but he uses it as his own personal possession. The same accusation could be made against some officials in our own day. But since John always kept his eye on Judas, we can accept his statement.

Meanwhile, many Jews learn that Jesus is present at the banquet and they hasten to see him out of curiosity and also to see and touch Lazarus, for they knew that he had been raised from the dead. Finding him alive among the living, we would expect a mass conversion. But no! Resurrection from the dead is not a sufficient motive for conversion for everyone.

On the contrary, when the chief priests see that the resurrection of Lazarus has become a possible means of proselytism for Jesus, they immediately think of killing Lazarus. For them it would be simply a question of preserving good order. It would be putting things back in their proper place. The living with the living, the dead with the dead. If the resurrected Lazarus is removed from their midst, the people will soon forget about the affair. They will begin to think that Lazarus did not truly rise from the dead. That manner of reasoning should make one smile, or even laugh out loud.[7]

---

[7] In Mt 26:6-13 and in Mk 14:3-9 the incident is described as occurring in the house of Simon the Leper.

Jesus Forgives a Public Sinner

Simon the Pharisee invites Jesus to dine with him,
but he soon shows himself to be a poor host.
A sinful woman, known to all as such, treats
Jesus with much greater kindness.

From the Gospel according to Luke (7:36-50):

Now one of the Pharisees asked Jesus to eat
with him, so he went into the Pharisee's house
and reclined at table. There was a woman who
was a sinner in the city, and when she learned
that "he's reclining at table in the Pharisee's
house!" she bought an alabaster jar of perfumed
oil and stood behind by his feet, weeping, and
she began to wet his feet with her tears and wipe
them with the hair of her head, and she kissed
his feet repeatedly and anointed them with the
oil.

Now when the Pharisee who had invited him
saw this he said to himself, "If this fellow were a
prophet he'd have realized who and what kind
of woman it is who's touching him — she's a sinner!"

In response Jesus said to him. "Simon, I have
something to say to you." And he said, "Teacher,
say it." "Two men were debtors of a certain mon-

eylender; the one owed five hundred denarii, the other, fifty. When they were unable to repay, he forgave them both. Which of them, then, will love him more?"

In answer Simon said, "I suppose the one he forgave the most." So he said to him, "You've judged correctly." And turning to the woman he said to Simon, "You see this woman?

I came into your house —
    you gave me no water for my feet,
But she wet my feet with her tears
    and dried them with her hair.
You gave me no kisses,
    but she, from the moment she came in,
        has not stopped kissing my feet.
You didn't anoint my head with olive oil,
    but she anointed my feet with perfumed oil.
Therefore I tell you: her sins, many as they are,
        have been forgiven,
    and so she has shown great love;
But whoever is forgiven little,
    loves little."

Then he said to her, "Your sins are forgiven." And those reclining at table began to say to themselves, "Who is this fellow who even forgives sins?" Then he said to the woman, "your faith has saved you, go in peace."

Jesus is invited to dine with the Pharisee Simon, more out of curiosity because of the fame of the Master than out of faith. Good and virtuous men are invited more to be shown to the world in one's home than to honor them. And in the East in those days, when a guest was invited to one's home, he was almost always an illustrious person, though it may also happen that uninvited guests appear. The latter are there simply as spectators, to look and listen. The custom is so deep-rooted that persons of every type and class may take advantage of it.

The meal is already under way in Simon's home. The dining room is large and sumptuous. Many of the invited guests are dressed in fine clothes. It is a festive affair and there is no regard for the cost. But all of a sudden one person exchanges knowing glances with another. They have noticed a woman standing against the wall. She is known to all as a sinner, possibly a prostitute. As people are staring at her, she suddenly moves. She has in her hands an alabaster vase filled to the brim with perfume. She falls at the feet of Jesus and begins to bathe them with her tears. Then she dries them with her hair, kisses them, and anoints them with the perfume.

The incident cannot pass without notice; it arouses a lively curiosity in the guests. Simon is not only deeply disturbed; he is thinking thoughts that must make Jesus smile.

We are witnessing a great human drama, the kind that can change a person's life forever. The woman is asking pardon, and perhaps at that very moment she is forgiven for her life of sin. In fact, she suddenly feels her spirits soar. Her tears are now at the same time tears of repentance and tears of joy.

And Simon, what is he thinking? This is what runs through his mind: if his illustrious guest is truly a prophet, he should know the type of woman who is touching him and anointing him with perfume. According to Simon's thinking, if Jesus is truly a prophet, he should stand up, scandalized, and eject that woman who, as everybody knows, is a consummate sinner.

For his part, perhaps, Jesus is wondering how these men can think that way. Surely, it makes him smile. But he likes Simon. He looks at him now as if he were a child, and he speaks to him the way a grown-up does when exerting authority. "Simon," he says, "I have something to say to you." Feeling highly honored to be singled out, Simon gives Jesus his complete attention, expecting, perhaps, some kind of special revelation.

Jesus now tells him the wonderful parable about the generous creditor who cancels the debt of two distinct debtors. It is a parable of great consolation to all of humanity.

Simon answers correctly when he says that the debtor for whom much more has been cancelled will love the creditor more. But the discussion does not end there, as perhaps the Pharisee would have wished. Jesus smiles to himself as thinks about what he is going to say to him in a moment. He is going to point out very emphatically how differently he was received in this house by the Pharisee, who is the host, and by the sinful woman. Simon had not even offered him water to wash his feet; he had not given him a welcoming kiss; he had not anointed his head with perfumed oil. No, the Pharisee had invited him out of curiosity, not out of love. The woman, on the other hand, had bathed his feet with her tears and dried them with her hair. She kept kissing his feet and anointing them with perfume. Consequently, she is the one who loves him more, because she has received forgiveness for her many sins.

We would think that the incident would conclude with the Master's words, so full of mercy and hope: "Your sins are forgiven." But no; there is more to come. The people at table ask each other: "Who is this fellow who even forgives sins?"

But Jesus pays no attention to their comments, which are a proof of the hardness of their hearts. Instead, he says to the woman: "Your faith has saved you, go in peace."

Fear Caused by a Miracle

In the region of the Gerasenes, a man possessed by a
legion of devils comes to be exorcised and cured
by Jesus, who transfers the devils from
the man to a herd of swine that are pasturing on the
mountainside. The people are more frightened than
impressed, and they ask Jesus to leave their region.

From the Gospel according to Luke (8:26-39):

Then they sailed to the region of the
Gerasenes, which is opposite Galilee. Now as he
was coming ashore a certain man from the city
who had a demon confronted him. This man
hadn't worn a cloak for a long time; he didn't live
in a house but instead lived among the tombs.
When he saw Jesus he cried out and fell down
before him and said in a loud voice, "What do
you want with me, Jesus, Son of the Most High
God? I beg you, don't torment me!" because he'd
been commanding the unclean spirit to come out
of the man.

Many times it had seized him, and he was
kept under guard and bound with chains and leg
irons, and when he'd break the chains he was
driven into the deserts by the demon. So Jesus
asked him, "What's your name?" "Legion," he

said, because many demons had gone into him. And they begged him not to order them to go off to the abyss.

Now there was a herd there of a considerable number of swine, feeding on the hillside, and when they begged him to let them go into them he let them. When the demons went out of the man they went into the swine, and the herd rushed down the slope into the lake and drowned.

Now when the herdsmen saw what had happened they fled and told those who were in the city and the fields. When the people went out to see what had happened and came to Jesus they found the man from whom the demons had gone out — clothed and in his right mind — seated at Jesus' feet, and they became frightened. Then those who had seen [what happened] told them how the demon-possessed man had been saved. And the whole crowd from the district of the Gesarenes asked him to go away from them, because they were seized with a great fear. So he got into a boat and returned. Now the man from whom the demons had gone out begged to stay with Jesus, but he sent him off and said, "Return to your house and announce what God has done for you." And he went off through the whole city, proclaiming what Jesus had done for him.

In the region of the Gerasenes, across from Galilee, the day is bathed in sunshine and the heat of the sun. Gazing at the blue sky, one is lost in its depths. A naked man presents himself to Jesus. Everybody knows him; they know that he is possessed by devils. On more than one occasion the people had tried to restrain him by putting him in chains, but to no avail. He always managed to free himself. No one could ever figure out where he got such great strength.

The man had no home, he lived among the tombs in the cemetery. Frequently he would be carried off to the desert by the demons that dwell there. Day and night he would shout and make a disturbance, beating on his chest with a stone. It had come to the point that nobody paid much attention to him anymore; he was now part of the regional folklore.

Matthew reports a similar episode , but it concerns two possessed men rather than one. They are from the vicinity of the town of Gadara, about twelve kilometers southeast of Tiberias (Mt 8:28-34). Mark, on the other hand, describes an incident that is similar to that described by Luke, but we know that in writing his Gospel, Mark borrowed copiously from Luke (cf. Mk 5:1-20).

In any case, the possessed man presents himself to Jesus but it is not he who speaks to Jesus; it is the devil, who possesses him. He recognizes Jesus as the Son of the Most High God and asks him not to torment him. Perhaps Jesus smiles. Look who recognizes me immediately and without delay! There are many who do not know who the Master really is; even among his disciples there are those who are doubtful. But his enemy the devil has no doubts. He knows with whom he is speaking. He is certain of it. He is surely a demon of lower rank; he humbles himself and asks for pity.

Jesus wants to unmask him in front of everybody. He asks his name. The demon responds cryptically that his name is "Legion." Jesus smiles knowingly. He realizes that he is not dealing with only one demon but with a great number of demons. One has answered in the name of all, but there are many demons who have taken up residence in that poor man, who lives naked among the tombs and cries out night and day.

Once they have been discovered, the demons beg Jesus in unison not to cast them into hell before time but to wait until the final judgment, as has been ordained. In a word, they are not anxious to join their leader in the world to which they have been condemned.

Jesus listens in silence. All things considered, he finds the situation really comical. There is a brief pause. Meanwhile the demons notice the herd of swine feeding on the hillside. After a quick consultation they ask Jesus to permit them to enter into those animals rather than being sent where they belong. Jesus consents. To each his own!

The unclean spirits (two thousand of them according to Mark) finally decide to leave the poor unfortunate man who against his will had been their host. One can imagine what happened to the swine when the demons entered into them. Just a while ago they were grazing in the sun or in the shade of the trees. Now, all of a sudden, they are terrorized, as if struck by a gigantic bolt of lightning. They dash headlong, one after the other, and jump off the precipice into the lake.

After such a din and confusion, things quiet down. The disappointment of the herdsmen is great. On the eastern shore of the lake live many inhabitants who are not Jews, so they eat pork. The herdsmen look toward the lake in astonishment: two thousand head of swine lost in the water. Little by little the herdsmen gather their wits together and then, thoroughly frightened, they hurry to the town and villages to report what happened.

Many people begin to arrive, curious to find out who caused this disaster. Jesus carefully observes what is happening. The newly arrived people pay no attention to the man who used to shout all the time and until recently was in the possession of the demons. They give him only a passing glance. They notice that he is fully dressed, calm and recovered. Then another fear begins to rise among them. It is a situation more than sufficient to make Jesus smile. Many men care more about material possessions and animals than about eternal life.

Then there are descriptions and reports from those who were present during the event, and questions and requests for information on the part of those who have just recently arrived. Jesus watches and waits. He knows that the crowd will not applaud and acclaim him.

As a matter of fact, the people who were present from the beginning do not even give an account of the fact that Jesus had worked a miracle on behalf of the poor possessed man. The question doesn't even arise, whether or not they believe in him. They all look on in silence, and suddenly they realize that they all have the same thought. The bolder ones express the thought: they ask Jesus to go away from there. They are scared to death and afraid that he might cause demons to invade other animals that are found in those parts.

Jesus shakes his head; he has to listen to this, too. But he does not argue; he gets into the boat to depart. The man who was freed from the evil spirits asks Jesus to take him along. Jesus smiles; there is at least one person who acknowledges him. But he does not take the man with him. Rather, he wants him to go back home and tell everybody about the gift he has received from God. And that's what the man did.

Martha the Domestic;
Mary the Devout

During a visit from Jesus at Bethany, Martha and her sister Mary manifest opposite attitudes toward housework. Jesus expresses himself regarding their differences and his judgment is unexpected and disconcerting.

From the Gospel according to Luke (10:38-42):

Now in their journeying he came into a certain village where a woman named Martha received him. She had a sister named Mary who seated herself at the Lord's feet and listened to his teaching. But Martha was distracted with all the serving, so she came up and said, "Lord, doesn't it matter to you that my sister has left me to serve alone?" In answer the Lord said to her, "Martha, Martha! You're anxious and upset over many things, but one thing is necessary. Mary has chosen the better part, which will not be taken from her."

This family discussion, which took place in the home of the friends of Jesus in Bethany, is frequently repeated in all homes. There are always some who work and others who prefer to visit with the guest.

In this case, however, the guest is someone excep-
tional.

It is not difficult, therefore, to imagine Martha
busy working, making sure that there are enough
plates for everyone and that the guests (Jesus with
some of his disciples) lack nothing, while Mary hap-
pily listens to the words of the Master. Divine words!
We also would have chosen that behavior. Martha,
on the other hand, is kept busy with domestic
chores. She is getting tired and she makes signs to
her sister to help her. But Mary is too comfortable,
sitting there and listening to Jesus. Maybe Mary
doesn't even notice that Martha needs her help.

Nothing escapes the attention of Jesus. He
smiles when he notices the unsuccessful efforts of
Martha to attract the attention of her sister. Meanwhile, he continues to talk and Mary doesn't miss a
word. From those words she garners a treasure that
is constantly increasing.

Jesus smiles again when he observes that Mary
is not even noticing that her sister is doing all the
work. And he knows that it is good that it should
be so. But Martha cannot stand it any longer. Exas-
perated, she finally decides to appeal directly to
Jesus to intervene and call Mary to order.

Once again Jesus is scolded. It has been somewhat frequent during his earthly sojourn. The im-
pertinence of his creatures! However, he does intervene. We would expect a very gentle intervention
in favor of Martha. "Mary," we imagine him saying,

"look at your sister, how hard she is working. Give her a hand. You'll finish the work earlier. She also has a right to sit and visit with us."

But no; according to Jesus, Martha goes to extremes. She is too much absorbed in material concerns and therefore she is the one who should be corrected and told to calm down. "Martha, Martha, haven't you yet learned that some things are more important than domestic work?"

Martha's face must surely have expressed astonishment. But Jesus smiles. "It may take some time, but you also will understand the meaning of my words."

Zacchaeus Climbs a Tree

The wealthy Zacchaeus, head of the Publicans,
was short of stature, so he climbed up a sycamore tree so
that he could see Jesus. Noticing this, Jesus tells
Zacchaeus that he will stop at his house this very day.

From the Gospel according to Luke (19:1-10):

Then he went in and passed through Jericho.
and, behold, a man named Zacchaeus was there;
he was chief tax collector and he was rich. He
was trying to see who Jesus was, but he wasn't
able to because of the crowd, because he was
short of stature. So he ran on ahead to the front
and climbed up into a sycamore in order to see
him, because he was going to be passing by
there.

When Jesus came to that place he looked up
and said to him, "Zacchaeus! Hurry on down! —
Today I must stay at your house!" So he hurried
down and welcomed him joyfully. When everyone saw this they complained and said, "He went
in as the guest of a sinful man!" But Zacchaeus
stood up and said to the Lord, "Look, Lord, I'm
giving half of my possessions to the poor, and if
I've cheated anyone of anything I'm paying back
fourfold." Then Jesus said to him, "Today salva-

tion has come to this house, because he's a son
of Abraham, too. For the Son of Man came to
seek out and save what was lost."

The name "Zacchaeus" can mean "the pure
one" or "Yahweh is remembered." The person by this
name described by Luke is a leader of the Publicans,
who are commissioned by the Romans as tax collectors. He is therefore a man who doesn't care much
for subtlety. He oppresses his fellow citizens without mercy in order to profit from the percentage that
he receives for the money he collects.

It's a good life but the price he pays for his
comfort and profit is that everyone considers him a
sinner. Nobody wants him in their home; everyone
avoids him. In addition, Zacchaeus is a very short
man and doesn't have a pleasing appearance. In
those days wealth alone was not enough to make a
man handsome and intelligent even if he is ugly.
That is a an achievement of our times.

Jesus is about to pass through Jericho, an important city in that region. He is well known every-
where; the fame of his teaching and his prodigies
precede him and accompany him.

Zacchaeus is curious; he wants to see this Jesus,
listen to him, find out in person who he really is. But
he doesn't want to — or cannot — enter the homes
of other people. So he tries to look over the heads
of the crowd that surrounds Jesus. He stands on the
tips of his toes and even leaps up in order to see,
but it's useless. A person in front of him looks haugh-

tily at his unsuccessful attempts. Zacchaeus pays no attention to him, but keeps trying. To no avail. In front of him there is too high a wall of heads and shoulders. Now he puts his mind to work: he knows that he is clever and creative. A sudden idea! He runs ahead of the crowd, climbs a sycamore tree and waits for Jesus to pass by.

Surely the thoughts of Zacchaeus and his tactics do not escape the notice of Jesus. He smiles with amusement. He knows that Zacchaeus is only curious. But he also knows that in a few moments the despised leader of the Publicans will become part of God's plan of redemption.

Zacchaeus must look comical up in the sycamore, trying not to lose his balance and fall out of the tree. That would be a pleasant diversion for everyone. He is holding on tightly to a thick branch and from time to time the leaves rustle noisily as he shifts his weight.

At last Jesus is passing under the tree. Zacchaeus has eyes only for him. His heart is in his throat. But what's happening? Jesus is looking up! Zacchaeus looks from one side to the other; there's no one else in the sycamore tree. "Jesus is looking right at me," he says to himself, overwhelmed with joy.

"Zacchaeus! Hurry on down! — Today I must stay at your house!"

Zacchaeus leaps right out of his skin! "He is really looking right at me," he says again, incredulous, "and he said that he is coming to my house!"

Jesus smiles, and we also smile when we read this Gospel passage. We would like to be on that tree in place of Zacchaeus. Jesus, who is eternal and beyond the limits of time, smiles and sees each one of us on that sycamore, if we so desire. "Do you really wish it?" he asks us. "Then come down and go home and get ready because today you will have me as your guest."

And that is not all. The crowd doesn't want to be deprived of the presence of Jesus, so they complain that Zacchaeus is a sinner and the Messiah should not go with him.

But the crowd does not understand. After such a long period of preaching, Jesus is still misunderstood. And it is that way today. There are always some persons who think they are better than others in God's sight. Jesus must be smiling and shaking his head when faced with these presumptuous fools.

Zacchaeus, on the other hand, understands everything quickly and acts on it. He announces that he will be generous with the poor and those whom he has cheated.

In all times, including our own, there is no more convincing proof of the sincerity of the good intentions of a person than to open one's purse, which is usually tightly closed. And the rich man, small of stature and leader of the Publicans, knows that very well.

According to the rabbinic law, the highest voluntary donation to the poor is set at one fifth of one's cash credit and one fifth of one's income. If anyone gives beyond the established limit, he must make restitution for the surplus, plus one fifth or at most one fourth. Zacchaeus is exaggerating: he says he will give half of his wealth to the poor and four-fold to anyone he has cheated.

Jesus smiles at this example of intelligence and generosity. And once again he tells those present that he has come down to earth especially for sinners. That is very consoling.

Healing of a Man Born Blind

With a bit of earth and saliva Jesus heals a man who is
blind from birth. When the parents are questioned
by the Pharisees, they are prudent and reticent.
But not the man born blind, who now finds himself in
good shape in every sense of the word. Not only does he
not deny that he was miraculously cured by Jesus, but
when the Pharisees press him, he retorts with irony.

From the Gospel according to John (9:1-34):

As he passed along he saw a man who was
blind from birth. The disciples asked him,
"Rabbi, who sinned, this fellow or his parents,
that he should be born blind?" Jesus answered.
"Neither he nor his parents sinned, but he was
born blind so that the works of God might be
revealed through him! We must do the works of
the One Who sent me while it's day; when night
comes, no one is able to work. As long as I'm in
the world, I'm the light of the world."

Having said these things he spit and made
clay out of the spittle, and he smeared the clay
on his eyes and said to him, "Go wash yourself
in the pool of Siloam," which is translated "Sent."
So he went off and washed himself and came
back seeing. His neighbors and those who used

to see him as a beggar said, "Isn't this the man who used to sit and beg?" Some said, "It is him!" others said, "No, it's not! but he's similar to him!" He said, "I'm the one!" So they said to him, "How were your eyes opened?" He answered, "The man called Jesus made clay and smeared it on my eyes and said to me, 'Go to Siloam and wash your-self!' When I went off and washed myself I could see." And they said to him, "Where is he?" He said, "I don't know."

They brought him to the Pharisees — the man who was formerly blind. Now it was the Sabbath on the day Jesus made the clay and opened his eyes. Once again they as well as the Pharisees asked him how it was that he could see. But he said, "He put clay on my eyes and I washed myself and now I can see." So some of the Pharisees said, "This man isn't from God because he doesn't keep the Sabbath!" Others said, "How can a sinful man do such signs?" And there was a split among them. So they said to the blind man again, "What do you say about him since it was your eyes he opened?" Then he said, "He's a prophet!"

The Jews didn't believe that the man had been blind and had gained his sight until they called the parents of the man who was now able to see and questioned them and said, "Is this your son, the one you say was born blind? How can he now see?" His parents answered, "We know that this is our son and that he was born blind, but how he can now see we don't know, nor do we know who opened his eyes. Ask him, he's of age!

He'll speak for himself!" His parents said these things because they were afraid of the Jews, for the Jews had already agreed that if anyone declared him to be the Messiah he'd be banished from the synagogue. Therefore, his parents said, "He's of age, ask him!"

So for a second time they called the man who had been blind and said to him, "Give glory to God! We know this man's a sinner!" He answered, "Whether he's a sinner, I don't know. One thing I do know — I was blind but now I can see." So they said to him, "What did he do to you? How did he open your eyes?" He answered them, "I've already told you but you didn't listen. Why do you want to hear again? Surely you don't want to become his disciples, too, do you."

Then they began to insult him and said, "You're his disciple, but we're Moses' disciples. We know that God spoke to Moses, but we don't know where this fellow's from." The man answered, 'The wonder is certainly in this, that you don't know where he comes from, yet he opened my eyes. We know God doesn't listen to sinners, but if anyone is God-fearing and does His will He listens to him. It hasn't been heard of from all eternity that someone opened the eyes of a man blind from birth. If this man weren't from God, he wouldn't have been able to do anything." They answered, "You were completely born in sin, and you're teaching us?" And they threw him out.

Jesus is usually concerned about spiritual blindness but he also occupies himself with physical blindness,[8] considering it one of the more serious afflictions.

Some winter evening turn out all the lights in your room and close your eyes tightly. Then start to walk. Every piece of furniture, every wall becomes an obstacle. They seem to be so hostile that they attack you! Voices heard from other rooms seem to be a source of salvation, but you are unable to get to them. You give up and remain in your room. You try to familiarize yourself with the world in the dark. Your groping hands try to touch a chair or the edge of the bed. They were within easy reach before you closed your eyes. Now there's just empty space. But at last you succeed in sitting down, and you think! This may give you some faint idea of what it is like to be blind.

But a person who is blind from birth has no recollection of anything visible that could be of help. So Jesus is walking down the road. Along the way he sees the bright red color of the pomegranates and the yellow flowers of the rue. On the way he meets a man who is blind since birth. Unlike Jesus, the disciples are not much concerned about the man's affliction. They simply ask Jesus who is to blame for the man's unfortunate condition — the

---

[8] Cf. Mt 9:27-31; 12:22; 20:29-34; Mk 8:22-26.

blind man himself or his parents. "Rabbi, whose sin is it?"

Jesus shakes his head; he always has to have patience. So much patience! Since there were no known cures for most of the diseases and afflictions in those times, people consoled themselves with the thought that they were the result of some sin, whether real or presumed. If a sickness or disease (or rather, the punishment) is diagnosed, there must necessarily have been some sin committed. But are we any different today?

Jesus permits the question, but the response that he gives doesn't leave room for any doubt: no one has sinned, neither the man or his parents. That affliction is part of the plan of God, so that men would believe in him, his Son.

Then, making a small bit of mud out of earth and his saliva, Jesus spreads it on the eyes of the blind man in order to dispel the darkness and replace it with the light. "Go wash yourself in the pool of Siloam," says Jesus. The man obeys, and when he returns he is able to see.

At this point there are a number of factors that bring a smile to the face of Jesus. Knowing full well that the restoration of one's sight is not an everyday occurrence, some of the blind man's neighbors and many others who had frequently met him on the road, think at first that this cannot be the same person. "It's him; it's not him; it's someone who looks like him; no, it's not really him; I can guarantee it, he's my neighbor; at least twice a day I meet him on the road."

"It's really me!" exclaims the man excitedly, and his joy is so great that his looks and even his voice are unrecognizable. And now someone in the crowd asks him who it was that performed this wonder. Various persons urge him to speak up without hesitation. "The man they call Jesus," he responded. He then adds the details: the saliva; the earth; the fresh mud smeared on his eyelids; the command to go and wash himself in the pool of Siloam; the first vague images; the first colors — blue, yellow and green; his amazement at being able for the first time to see his hands, his body, his feet and... the world!

Pleased with the happiness of the man, Jesus smiles as he watches him jump up and down in the midst of the crowd that surrounds him, shouting:"I can see! I can see! I can see!" Some persons in the crowd do not share the happiness of the man who a short while ago was blind from birth and now has his sight. "Where is the man who did this?" they asked. "I don't know," he answered.

They then lead him to the Pharisees so that he can repeat to them what has happened. The man doesn't need to be coaxed. He again tells his story, this time perhaps with more details than the first time. And this immediately gives rise to a dispute: today is the Sabbath day; every kind of work is forbidden, even the task of mixing a small amount of mud. Much less is it permitted to work a miracle! The diatribe makes them appear both ludicrous and ridiculous!

So at once they try to save face by asking the man: "What do you say about him, now that he has opened your eyes?" "He is a prophet," is the prompt reply. The Pharisees shake their heads. The cure has gone to his head! Better to get precise information from his parents. but the parents immediately become extremely submissive and timid in front of the powerful Pharisees. Then as now the poor eat their bread with prudence and fear.

"We know that this is our son," says the father, casting a glance at his wife. "We also know that he was blind and now he can see," the father adds, but a bit uneasy at not finding the expected reassurance in the eyes of his wife. "But we don't know who has given him sight or how. Why don't you ask him? We were not there. He is grown up and he is not out of his mind," says the father, and his wife nods in agreement.

At this point the Pharisees call back the man who had been blind and they repeat the same questions. After listening to the man's repeated testimony, they assert that Jesus cannot be anything else but a sinner. The happiness at receiving his sight gives the cured man an unexpected boldness. He now addresses the Pharisees with a subtle irony: "Whether or not he's a sinner, I don't know. But I do know for sure that I was blind and now I can see. For my part I have already explained everything.

Why do you want me to repeat the same things to you? Could it be that you also want to become his disciples?"

At these words Jesus cannot help but smile with amusement. But the Pharisees are not amused; they react with very different feelings, declaring that they are disciples of Moses, to whom God has spoken. As for Jesus, they don't know where he comes from or who he is.

The cured man does not let up: "It is really strange," he says. "You do not know where he comes from or who he is, but he opened my eyes." Then the man added: "It has never been heard that a sinner could give sight to the blind. Only God can work that miracle. Now we know that God does not listen to sinners, but if anyone is God-fearing and does his will, he listens to him."

It cannot end well for someone who speaks clearly. The man is thrown out of the synagogue. On the street he will again meet Jesus, who will again smile on seeing him. Then, in addition to the gift of sight, he will give the man the gift of faith.

The Resurrection of Lazarus

Lazarus is seriously ill. Jesus is told about it but he does
not immediately respond. The disciples cannot
understand his behavior. By the time Jesus arrives at
Bethany, Lazarus has been dead for four days.
Martha and Mary reproach him gently. Jesus restores
Lazarus to life because they believe.

From the Gospel according to John (11:1-44):

Now a certain man was sick, Lazarus of
Bethany, from the village of Mary and her sister
Martha. Mary was the one who had anointed the
Lord with oil and wiped his feet dry with her hair
— it was her brother Lazarus who was sick. So
the sisters sent to him and said, "Lord, behold,
the one you love is sick." When Jesus heard this
he said, "This sickness will not bring death —
it's for the glory of God so the Son of Man may
be glorified through it."

Now Jesus loved Martha and her sister and
Lazarus, but when he heard that Lazarus was sick
he stayed where he was for two more days. Then
after this he said to the disciples, "Let's go into
Judea again." The disciples said to him, "Rabbi,
the Jews were just trying to stone you, and now
you're going back there again?" Jesus answered,
"Aren't there twelve hours in a day?

If someone walks in the day he doesn't stumble,
      because he sees the light of this world.
But if someone walks in the night he stumbles,
      because the light isn't with him."

He said these things, and then he said to
them, "Our friend, Lazarus, has fallen asleep, but
I'm going now to wake him up." So the disciples
said to him, "Lord, if he's fallen asleep he'll recover." But Jesus had spoken about his death,
while they thought he was speaking about natu-
ral sleep. So then Jesus said to them openly,
"Lazarus has died, and I rejoice for your sakes
that I wasn't there, so you may believe." So Thomas, who was called the Twin, said to his fellow
disciples, "Let's go, too, so we can die with him."

When Jesus came he found that Lazarus had
already been in the tomb for four days. Now
Bethany was near Jerusalem, about two miles
away, and many of the Jews had come to Martha
and Mary to console them over their brother. So
Martha, when she heard that Jesus was coming,
met him, but Mary sat in the house. Martha said
to Jesus, "Lord, if you'd been here my brother
wouldn't have died! but even now I know that
whatever you ask God for, God will give you."
Jesus said to her, "Your brother will rise!" Martha
said to him. "I know that he'll rise at the resurrection on the last day." Jesus said to her,

"I am the resurrection and the life!
Whoever believes in me, even if he should die,
      will live.
And everyone who lives and believes in me
      shall never die!

Do you believe this?" She said to him, "Yes, Lord, I've come to believe that you're the Messiah, the Son of God who has come into the world!"

After she said these things she went off and called her sister Mary, saying quietly. "The Teacher is here and he's asking for you." When she heard that, she got up quickly and went to him. Now Jesus had not yet come to the village, but was still at the place where Martha had met him. So the Jews who were with her in the house, consoling her — when they saw that Mary had quickly gotten up and gone out — they followed her, thinking, "She's going to the tomb to weep there."

When Mary came to where Jesus was and saw him she fell at his feet and said to him, "Lord, if you'd been here my brother wouldn't have died!" So when Jesus saw her weeping, and the Jews who had come with her weeping, he groaned in spirit and was troubled and he said, "Where have you laid him?" They said to him, "Lord, come and see!" Jesus began to weep. So the Jews said, "See how he loved him!" But some of them said, "Couldn't the one who opened the eyes of the blind man have caused this man not to die?"

So Jesus, again groaning within himself, came to the tomb. Now it was a cave, and a stone lay on it. Jesus said, "Take the stone away!" Martha, the sister of the dead man, said to him, "Lord, by now he'll smell — it's been four days!" Jesus said to her, "Didn't I tell you that if you believe you'll see the glory of God?" So they took the stone away.

Then Jesus lifted up his eyes and said, "Father, I give you thanks, because you heard me. Now I knew that you always hear me, but I said this for the sake of the crowd standing around me, so they may believe that you sent me." And after saying this he called out with a loud voice, "Lazarus, come out!" The dead man came out with his hands and feet bound with thongs and his face wrapped with a cloth. Jesus said to them, "Untie him and let him go!"

Because of its very dramatic content, I was not sure whether I should include this episode. We actually see that Jesus was so deeply moved that he wept. He will do so again only when he gazes upon Jerusalem (Lk 19:41). And this will be yet another manifestation of the completeness of the human nature of Jesus. However, we shall try to see this incident in the life of Jesus in a different light, one that is joyful.

In addition to his disciples, Jesus also had many friends. Among the latter were Lazarus and his sisters, Martha and Mary, who lived in Bethany, just a few miles distant from Jerusalem. And so at the time that the news came from the sisters of Lazarus that he was seriously ill, Jesus was not very far away. But he does not go immediately to his friend's side. The delay, however, must not be attributed to a lukewarm love for the three friends at Bethany, but rather to the fact that Jesus knows that events have to unfold in a manner quite different from the way that one would expect. It was thus decreed long ago: he is not to go to Bethany to cure a sick man, but for much more.

Besides, the two sisters are only hoping that he will come, but they do not explicitly ask him to come. So Jesus pacifies the messenger sent by Martha and Mary, assuring him that Lazarus will not die and that this sickness will serve as a testimony for the glory of God and his Son.

These words are not understood by those who are standing around him, and Jesus smiles frequently when he perceives the bewilderment in the eyes of those who love him. His disciples are what they are. He himself chose them. They don't rate high in intelligence. But can we perhaps presume that if the choices of Jesus had been different — if, for example, he had called to himself some of the intellectuals of his day — his words would have fallen on fertile ground? If we consider how the majority of intellectuals have treated Jesus throughout the centuries, we can seriously doubt it.

After spending two more days in the place where he was, Jesus decides to make the trip to Bethany in Judea. Once more the disciples reproach the Master. What is this? A few days ago the Jews wanted to stone you, and now you want to go into their territory? It is difficult to tolerate the presumption of the disciples, who even dare to reprimand Jesus. Instinctively we imagine that on this occasion also Jesus good-naturedly shakes his head and smiles.

But Jesus does not give up in the attempt to make them understand. He tries to do so with another statement. There are twelve hours in the day, he says, and twelve at night. If a person walks by day he can walk quickly, but if he walks at night, he may stumble and fall. Therefore for Jesus it is still daylight and he can walk wherever he wants without any danger.

He goes on to say that the hour has come for going to see his friend, Lazarus, because he is sleeping and must be awakened. Again the disciples understand only what they are able to understand or what they want to understand. They respond that Lazarus will surely get well because after a good sleep all the sick improve and get well. "Of course, Jesus, of course," they say. "We understood what you said. Don't you see that we are not that stupid?"

The important thing for them is to avoid traveling in Judea and perhaps be killed. The reassuring words of the Master do not really convince them. Some Jews don't joke! They mean what they say.

Jesus doesn't lose patience in the face of their objections He becomes more explicit. Lazarus has died. That was allowed to happen in order to strengthen their faith. At these words Thomas, famous throughout the ages for his stubborn incredulity, exclaims: "All right! Let's all go with him and let ourselves be killed as well!" Jesus surely shakes his head and smiles at this outburst. How difficult it is to make himself understood even by someone who loves him!

Well, then, Jesus is in Bethany. Lazarus has been in the tomb for four days. This is not an unusual circumstance; in the East it is customary to bury the dead on the very day of their death, because decomposition begins quickly. The son of the widow of Nain was being carried to the grave when Jesus restored him to life (Lk 7:11-17). The resurrection of the daughter of Jairus took place even earlier (Mt 9:18-26; Mk 5:22-43; Lk 8:41-56). But in the case of Lazarus, Jesus arrives on the scene four days after the death and burial.

According to popular belief among the Jews, the complete loss of life occurs only after the third day. At this point the face is no longer recognizable and the soul leaves the body. Until that moment the soul had hovered over the body. Therefore the resurrection of Lazarus was much more impressive.

Martha approaches Jesus and, after a veiled reprimand, she trusts in her faith. But when Jesus assures her that her brother will rise, look at the consummate lack of comprehension: "I know that he'll rise at the resurrection on the last day!" Jesus then proclaims his divinity: "I am the resurrection and the life! Whoever believes in me, even if he should die, will live, and everyone who lives and believes in me shall never die! Do you believe this?" The woman does not delay in responding: "Yes, Lord, I've come to believe that you're the Messiah, the Son of God, who has come into the world!" Then Martha runs to fetch Mary.

Jesus is still outside the village. Mary walks toward him, followed by all the Jews who are mourning with her. When she comes into his presence, she falls at his feet and, like her sister, she voices the same reproach: "Lord, if you'd been here my brother wouldn't have died!" Seeing her weep, and the Jews who accompany her, Jesus is deeply moved and he weeps also.

Then they all go together to the tomb of Lazarus. When Jesus commands that the stone be moved away from the cave, Martha intervenes again. She is worried about the stench that may come forth from the tomb.

Perhaps a patient smile returns to the face of Jesus. Look at what the woman is concerned about; think of it! Human sensitivity takes precedence over the solemnity of that which is about to take place.

Jesus addresses the Father and thanks him for this new miracle. He knows that as a result of the resurrection of his dear friend, many will believe in him. But not all!

"Lazarus, come out!" he commands in a loud voice. And Lazarus comes out of the tomb, still wrapped in the funeral linens, his face covered by the shroud. Jesus orders the people present to free Lazarus from these last remnants of the grave and let him go free. He smiles as he sees the happiness of his friend at being returned to life in this world. But perhaps it is a veiled smile because he knows that since Lazarus has been raised from the dead, eventually he will have to die a second time.

Three Booths on the Mountain

The ingenuous Peter suggests to Jesus that three booths
be constructed on the mountain; one for him,
one for Moses, and one for Elijah. But as soon as they
hear the voice proclaim Jesus the beloved Son of God,
Peter and the two brothers, James and John,
fall to the ground, overcome with fear.

From the Gospel according to Matthew (17:1-9):

Six days later Jesus took Peter and James and
his brother John along and led them up a high
mountain by themselves. And he was trans-
formed in front of them and his face shone like
the sun, while his clothing became as white as
light. And behold, Moses appeared to them as
well as Elijah, and they were speaking with him.
So in response Peter said to Jesus, "Lord, it's good
for us to be here; if you wish, I'll put up three
dwellings here, one for you, one for Moses, and
one for Elijah."

While he was still speaking, behold a bright
cloud overshadowed them and, behold, a voice
from the cloud said, "This is my Beloved Son, in
whom I am well pleased, hear him!" When the
disciples heard it they fell on their faces and were
overwhelmed with fear, but Jesus came and

touched them and said, "Get up; don't be afraid any more!" And when they raised their eyes they saw no one but Jesus alone.

As they were descending the mountain Jesus commanded them, "Tell no one the vision until the Son of Man has risen from the dead."

This incident is also reported by Mark (Mk 9:2-13) and Luke (Lk 9:28-36), but it is curious that John does not speak of it, although he was a direct witness.

After having revealed to Peter and the other two disciples his imminent passion, death and resurrection, Jesus invites Peter, James and John to accompany him on a high mountain. The evangelists report the choice of Peter, James and John without any comment. There is no indication of any jealousy on the part of those disciples who were not invited, and Matthew was one of them. Jesus is able to favor some friendships over others without excluding anyone from salvation and glory.

Jesus and the three disciples set off on a long walk, up the high mountain. They leave behind them the stretches of green vineyards, then the trees, and finally the ground becomes stony and arid. Most likely the three disciples are chatting among themselves, especially commenting on the latest revelations received from the Master. Or perhaps they are concentrating on their own thoughts and the prospect of a not too rosy future.

When they reach the summit, Jesus betakes

himself to prayer while the three disciples give in to weariness and fall asleep. But soon they are awakened by a brilliant light that emanates from the face of Jesus. It is a light as bright and intense as that of the sun. His clothing is resplendent with a whiteness that has never before been seen. "What's happening?" the disciples ask. Then all of a sudden they see Moses and Elijah conversing with Jesus. According to Luke's account, they were speaking with Jesus about his "Exodus, which he would bring to completion in Jerusalem" (9:31). The vision must have been marvelous, ecstatic.

Peter is delirious with joy. With his customary boldness mixed with rashness, which prompts him to turn to Jesus in a confidential manner (sometimes to utter a complaint), he asks Jesus if he should construct three dwellings, one for each of the three, so that they can prolong their miraculous presence together and enjoy their mutual euphoria.

Jesus surely smiles at Peter's ingenuity. The apostle to whom he has entrusted his Church on earth has not yet understood that man's redemption has already started in human history. It cannot be stopped; however painful, it must run its course until it is finished.

Peter, James and John are still dazed by the transfiguration of Jesus when a luminous cloud overshadows and envelops them. They are paralyzed with fear. And before they can understand what is happening to them now, from inside the cloud comes the voice of the Father, who tells them to listen to the words of his Beloved Son. This is too much for the three disciples. They fall to the earth with their faces to the ground; they have lost control over their legs as well as their minds.

Jesus is somewhat surprised at their behavior and he smiles again at seeing them overwhelmed by fear in spite of the fact that he is with them. That voice is known to him and there is no reason to be afraid of it. "It is the Father," he tells the three disciples. They can do nothing. They can't get hold of themselves. What is happening is just too much for them.

Jesus touches them and encourages them. "Get up!" he tells them with a smile on his lips. "Don't be afraid!" The three disciples look up but they see no one but Jesus. Moses and Elijah are no longer there.

A little later, as they go down the mountain, Jesus asks them not to speak to anyone about the apparition, "until the Son of Man has risen from the dead." John surely has faith in that promise; so why did he experience such great fear?

Jesus Succeeds Where
the Disciples Fail

After the transfiguration, Jesus, Peter, James and John
rejoin the others. A man steps out of the crowd and
carries to Jesus his epileptic son, whom the
disciples of Jesus had been unable to cure.

From the Gospel according to Matthew (17:14-21):

And as they were coming toward the crowd
a man came up to him, knelt before him, and
said, "Lord, have mercy on my son. He's epileptic and suffers terribly — many times he falls into
the fire and many times into the water. I brought
him to your disciples, but they couldn't cure
him."

In answer Jesus said,

"O unbelieving and perverse generation!
How long will I be with you?
How long will I put up with you?
Bring him here to me!"

Jesus rebuked the demon and it went out of
him, and the child was cured from that very hour.
Then the disciples came to Jesus privately and
said, "Why couldn't we drive it out?" But he said
to them, "Because of your weak faith, for, truly,

I say to you, if you have faith like a grain of mustard seed you'll say to this mountain, "Move from here to there!" and it will move, and nothing will be impossible for you. [But this type doesn't come out except through prayer and fasting]."

After the transfiguration, which was witnessed by Peter, James and John, Jesus rejoins his other disciples. The heavens are blue and there is not a cloud in the sky. The ground reflects the heat of the sun and the people seem to be enjoying themselves. As usual, a crowd is waiting for Jesus, a crowd attracted by the wonders worked by Jesus and wanting to see him and greet him.

Suddenly a man steps out from the rest of the crowd. He is a father, and he has a sick son, an epileptic. He is desperate because nobody can do anything to cure his boy. He prostrates himself at the feet of Jesus, knowing that this is his last hope. But he also knows that all the others who have asked for help with sincerity and devotion have been heard. On his knees and out of his sorrow as a father he begs for mercy for his son. As if it were necessary, he describes to the Master the symptoms of the disease. During an attack the boy sometimes falls into the fire or into the water, where he thrashes around violently. He suffers terribly. At the end of his petition he makes a statement that makes Jesus smile: "I brought him to your disciples, but they couldn't cure him."

That must have caused a bit of embarrassment and irritation among the disciples. How dare he! We did our best but without success. And now? Does he have to make this known in public?

Jesus reacts in a manner that is at once severe and paternal. First of all he reprimands those present — and also those absent — for their lack of faith, This is something that is a constant test of his patience. Immediately afterwards he commands that the boy be brought to him. It is not difficult for him to drive out the demon that possessed the boy. He does so with a few words of rebuke and the boy is immediately cured.

The second part of the incident likewise causes Jesus to smile. The disciples most likely did not feel as happy about the cure as they should have. They are not satisfied with being participants in the success of the Master. So they call Jesus aside and ask him: "Why couldn't we drive it out, while you did it with the greatest of ease?"

This is almost risking a repetition of the original sin! How is that you succeed, God, and we do not? But Jesus knows that those disciples of his have already experienced the weight of original sin on their backs, so he does not react harshly. Rather, he is somewhat amused at their behavior, so he explains it to them: "Because of your weak faith."

He then admonishes them again with a very beautiful statement, one that gives hope to all, and even to those who think they do not have it: "If you have faith like a grain of mustard seed you'll say to this mountain: 'Move from here to there!' and it will move, and nothing will be impossible for you."

These words satisfy the disciples. From that moment on, the pathway is open for making all things possible through a faith that is not extremely great but on the contrary is really small. But the disciples will soon learn the cost of a faith as small as a grain of mustard seed.

Paying Taxes

Jesus pays for himself and for Peter the annual
tax for the maintenance of the Temple.

From the Gospel according to Matthew (17:24-27):

When they came to Capernaum those who
were collecting the Temple tax came up to Peter
and said, "Doesn't your Teacher pay the Temple
tax?" "Certainly he does" he said. And when he
came into the house Jesus anticipated him by saying, "What do you think, Simon? The kings of the
earth — from whom do they collect tax or toll?
From their followers or from others?" And when
he said, "From others," Jesus said to him, "So then
their followers are exempt! But so we don't offend
them, go to the sea, cast a hook in, and take the
first fish that comes up, and when you open its
mouth you'll find a silver coin, worth twice the
Temple tax; take it and give it to them for me and
you."

This incident causes more than a smile in Jesus
and also in us. Matthew, a known tax collector, is
the only one of the evangelists to refer to taxes several times.[9]

---

[9] Mt 22:15-22; Mk 12:13-17; Lk 20:20-26.

It's a professional fixation! It is always to defend Jesus against the accusation that he is evading the payment of taxes, although in the passage concerning the payment of tribute to Caesar, the pretext of the Pharisees is not directed so much at tax evasion as an attempt to see "how they could entrap him in his speech" (Mt 22:15). Now on one occasion when Jesus and his disciples were at Capernaum, Peter was approached by the collectors of taxes for the maintenance of the Temple. They were aware of the relationship between Jesus and his disciples, but they do not deal directly with the interested party. Rather, the brave functionaries contact someone who is close to him. They find Peter outside the house and they ask him if his Master obeys the law governing payment of the Temple tax or not. We don't know if Peter was a bit fearful or apprehensive, but he answered without hesitation: "Certainly he does!" But maybe he is exempt; there seems to be a bit of confusion on this point.

When the tax collectors went on their way, Peter hurries into the house to report the bad news. To be questioned by the Commission on Finance is never a pleasant experience. But Jesus knows and he smiles at such fears. Just one more thing human beings have to put up with! Now he pacifies his right-hand man by opening the conversation with a question: he asks whether the children and family of a king are obliged to pay taxes to the sovereign. The answer is already contained in the question. Jesus, king of life and of the universe, cannot be reduced to the level of a taxpayer. It is truly an absurdity for tax collectors to ask God to pay taxes to them.

But Jesus saves everyone from embarrassment. He knows that his Kingdom is not of this world and he also knows that in coming to earth he becomes a man in every respect. So he offers Peter a solution "so we don't offend them." He tells him to go to Lake Tiberias and cast in a fish-hook. The first fish that he catches will have a silver coin in its mouth, sufficient to pay the tax for Jesus and also for Peter. Accustomed by this time to be asked to do unusual things and faithful in doing whatever the Master desires, Peter goes to the lake and casts the hook, without even having to overcome the slightest hesitation.

Jesus must surely smile when he looks at Peter's face as he takes the coin out of the mouth of the fish. Too bad that it has to be turned over to the tax collectors!

A Mother's Love

Mothers have blind spots when it comes to their children,
especially their sons. That is what happened to Salome,
the mother of James and John, the sons of Zebedee.

From the Gospel according to Matthew (20:20-28):

Then the mother of the sons of Zebedee came
up to him with her sons and knelt down to make
a request of him. So he said to her, "What do you
want?" She said to him, "Say that these two sons
of mine can sit, one at your right hand and one
at your left hand, in your Kingdom." But in answer Jesus said, "You don't know what you're
asking for. Can you drink the cup I'm going to
drink?" They said to him, "We can." He said to
them, "You will, indeed, drink my cup, but as for
sitting at my right hand or my left, that isn't mine
to give — it's for those for whom it's been prepared by my Father." And when the other ten
heard they became indignant at the two brothers. So Jesus called them together and said, "You
know that

The rulers of the Gentiles lord it over them.
And their leaders exercise authority over them,

but it won't be like that among you; instead,

Whoever would be great among you,
   let him be your servant,
And whoever would be first among you,
   let him be your slave;
Just as the Son of Man came, not to be served,
      but to serve;
   and to give his life as a ransom for many."

Luke reports this incident in an artificial manner, inserting it in the midst of a discussion about who is the greatest among them. Mark hands it down without the petition of the mother of the two beloved disciples. In fact, in Mark's account it is James and John who come to Jesus with the request: "Grant us that we may sit, one at your right hand and one at your left hand, in your glory" (Mk 10:37).

We do not know if these words would have prompted a smile on the face of Jesus more than the same request coming from the mother of the sons of Zebedee. To think that anyone would address God with such impudence is enough to arouse either indignation or pity. But Jesus is patient, so very patient.

I have chosen the version of Matthew for a consideration of this episode. According to him, Salome, the mother of James and John, approaches Jesus with great humility and prostrates herself in front of him. The other disciples are naturally surprised and curious. The silence is palpable. Perhaps the woman realizes that what she is about to request is a great deal, but it is for her two sons, and since they are sons, it is worth the trouble to assume any posture and present any request.

Jesus knows what the woman is about to ask of him, but nevertheless he queries her: "What do you want?" It is almost an attempt to make her reflect on what she is doing. Salome does not stop to think it over, but she is prudent nonetheless. She asks Jesus to "say," that is, to arrange in some way or in turn to ask his Father if her two sons can sit, one at his right and one at his left once they are in the kingdom.

It matters not that the people standing around can hear what she is saying, or that Jesus may think otherwise. In fact, she may be asking that privilege for her sons precisely in that place and at that moment so that it can be known to all, with hands outstretched, as if she is anticipating or can modify the plan of God.

Jesus smiles at the request of this mother. Perhaps many a mother, on the day of her son's ordination to the priesthood, has asked Jesus to make her son pope, or at least a bishop!

But Jesus then gives a gentle reprimand: "You don't know what you're asking for!" And he adds that only the Father can determine who will sit next to him, which one on the right and which one on the left.

Another reason for smiling presents itself a little later. On hearing the words of Jesus and on realizing their escape from the danger of being displaced at the request of Salome, the other ten disciples are angry at the two brothers. If the mother of James and John presented this request to Jesus, then her sons, the two brothers, must have consented to her action. It makes their tempers rise. The whole situation must impress the Master as ludicrous, but only up to a certain point. Jesus cuts short the discussion and admonishes those present: "Whoever would be great among you, let him be your servant; and whoever would be first among you, let him be your slave."

We can only imagine the expressions on the faces of Salome and her two sons. And perhaps we should look into our own hearts. Then Jesus will have to smile again!

The Naked Young Man

At Gethsemane, after the arrest of Jesus,
everybody flees, leaving him to his fate.
But a young man, wrapped only in a sheet, follows Jesus,
the group of soldiers and the representatives of the
Sanhedrin. The soldiers try to arrest the young man also,
but he breaks away, leaving them holding the sheet, as he
runs away naked. There is a good possibility that
the young man is Mark, the Evangelist.

From the Gospel according to Mark
(14:32; 14:42-52):

When they came to a place named
Gethsemane he said to his disciples, "Sit here
while I pray." He took Peter and James and John
along with him and he became very distressed
and troubled.... And right then, while he was
still speaking, Judas, one of the Twelve, arrived,
and with him a crowd with swords and clubs
from the chief priests and the scribes and the
elders. Now the one handing him over had given
them a sign, saying, "Whoever I kiss is the one,
seize him and lead him away under guard." Judas came right up to him and said. "Rabbi!" and
kissed him. So they laid hands on him and seized
him. Then one of those present drew his sword,

struck the high priest's slave, and cut off his ear. In answer Jesus said to them, "You came out with swords and clubs to seize me, as if you were after a robber? I was among you daily, teaching in the Temple, yet you didn't seize me; but let the scriptures be fulfilled." Then they all forsook him and fled.

A certain young man was following, wearing a linen cloth on his bare body, and they seized him, but he left the linen behind and fled naked.

Beyond the Cedron torrent there is a garden called Gethsemane. There one can see the gnarled trunks of centuries-old olive trees. In that Garden one of the most dramatic events in the history of the human race took place. And, like all human events, the drama was interspersed with moments of comedy.

Jesus feels the need to pray, but he does not want to involve all of the disciples. As on numerous other occasions, he takes with him only Peter, James and John. The Master is weighed down with anguish. His soul is sorrowful unto death. Not because of the death toward which he is advancing ever more rapidly, but because of the sin of humanity that is the cause of that death. The God who is sent is not acknowledged; his words are misunderstood; his life is sacrificed without any apparent redemption for anyone. The only human consolation for him at that moment must come from the three disciples whom he loves so much. That's why he invites them to come along with him and pray. Then he prostrates himself on the ground a little distance from them and begins to beg the Father that if it be possible these terrible moments might pass him by. The prayer ends with his total acceptance of the will of the Father.

When Jesus returns to the three beloved disciples, he finds them asleep. He smiles sadly. Peter, you haven't lasted for even an hour! You can fall asleep at a time like this! We can imagine the expression on the faces of Peter and the other two disciples.

Jesus moves away a second time in order to pray to the Father. When he returns to the three he again finds them asleep. This time he has to smile because Peter, James and John look at each other in search of a plausible excuse. They are at a loss for words.

When Jesus rejoins them a third time and finds his three disciples once more overcome by sleep, he does not even try to reprimand them. With a sad smile he shakes his head and lets them sleep and take their rest. But they don't enjoy it for long. Judas is arriving with an armed crowd to arrest Jesus. And now, look! It is the most infamous kiss in human history!

Peter does not hesitate (Jn 18:10-11). He draws his sword and in one stroke he cuts off the ear of Malchus, a servant of the high priest. Jesus immediately intervenes and restores the ear that had just been cut off (Lk 22:51). As God, he could have had on the spot twelve thousand legions of angels to come to his defense (Mt 26:53). So on seeing what men will contrive to do in a situation like this, he cannot help but smile and shake his head yet another time. But let the Scriptures be fulfilled.

One by one the disciples escape. Abandoned and standing alone, Jesus is surrounded by the soldiers and those who had been sent by the high priest. Exulting at their meaningless victory, the crowd leads Jesus out of the Garden of Gethsemane. None of his disciples follow him, even at a distance. No one, that is, except... the young Mark. Perhaps he had just got out of bed, awakened by the noise of the crowd, and he decides to stay close to Jesus.

The soldiers and the others see him. At first they pay no attention to him. Someone makes a gesture at him to go away. Mark pays no heed. He continues to follow. Then a pair of soldiers leave the group with the intention of arresting that impertinent young man. They don't exactly know why, but they'll begin by arresting him and then they'll see later. It's an age-old injustice and it's still practiced!

The young man immediately senses their intention and begins to move away. The soldiers pursue him and grab hold of the sheet which he has wrapped around him. But Mark is more agile than the soldiers. He leaves them holding the sheet as he dashes away stark naked, causing Jesus to smile with approval.

Peter's Denial

Peter, the leader of the disciples, repeatedly and forcefully proclaims his loyalty to Jesus, even if it costs him his life. But Jesus, who knows the human heart better than anyone, predicts that before the rooster crows twice, Peter will have denied him three times.

The Gospel according to Mark (14:27-31; 66-72):

Then Jesus said to them, "All of you will lose your faith, because it is written,

'I will strike the shepherd
and the sheep will be scattered'[10]

but after I rise I'll go ahead of you into Galilee." But Peter said to him, "Even if they all lose their faith, I won't!" Jesus said to him, "Amen, I say to you, today, this very night, before the rooster crows twice, you'll deny me three times." But Peter kept saying, "Even if it comes to dying with you, I won't deny you." And they all said the same, too....

While Peter was down in the courtyard one of the high priest's maidservants came, and when she saw Peter warming himself she looked right

---

[10] Cf. Zc 13:7.

at him and said, "You were with Jesus the Nazarene, too!" But he denied it and said, "I neither
know nor understand what you're saying!" And
he went outside into the gateway and a rooster
crowed.

When the maidservant saw him she again began to tell the bystanders, "This fellow's one of
them!" but he denied it again. After a little while
the bystanders again said to Peter, "Surely you're
one of them — you're a Galilean, too!" And he
put himself under a curse and swore an oath, "I
don't know the man you're talking about!" At that
moment a cock crowed a second time. Then
Peter remembered what had been said, how Jesus
had told him, "Before a cock crows twice you'll
deny me three times," and he stormed out weeping.

There is no son or daughter who in the early
years of life does not make use of expressions of
absolute love and utmost generosity in reference to
father and mother. "Mama, I wish you all good
things, the best in all the world." "You are the best
papa in the world." "I love you very much. Nothing
and no one will ever separate me from you." "When
I grow up I'm going to buy you a big house, with
servants and acres of land; we'll go horseback riding
every day." But then, in spite of dreams and promises, life takes over and follows its own course.

Although he is no longer a child, Peter acts like
one to some extent. He doesn't want to think of
anything that would put a limit on his great love for

Jesus. Let them put him in prison, torture him, kill him in a most cruel manner; nothing will ever dampen the ardor of his love.

Jesus surely smiles, in the same way that a parent smiles at the child's exaggerated statements and promises. Jesus is the one who best knows the human heart. The future is always before him, like an open book. He wants Peter to know in advance how difficult it is to believe in him and suffer for him. He predicts that it will not take cruel torture to make Peter deny him. All it will take is words from a woman and a few other persons standing around an open fire. Jesus already knows that Peter will deny the truth three times in the interval between the first and third crowing of the rooster. Although Peter protests and promises in good faith that he will always be a devoted disciple of Christ, events will prove once again that Jesus is right.

After the arrest of the Master and the hasty flight of the disciples from the Garden of Gethsemane, Peter and John follow the events at a safe distance — especially Peter (Jn 18:15-27), who prefers to remain near the gate. But John, who is known to the high priest, has no problem entering the courtyard where Jesus is. He even speaks with the young gatekeeper on behalf of Peter so that he, too, can enter the courtyard. How little Peter was pleased with this idea will be seen shortly.

In fact, as soon as the portress sees Peter, she immediately suspects that he is one of the follow-

ers of the arrested man. She asks him if he is, just to
verify her suspicion, and Peter pretends that he
doesn't know what she's talking about. John, meanwhile, is very calm, but Peter is afraid. It doesn't
augur well for the Master and his disciples. Better
to be prudent; better always to deny.

"But what is this woman talking about?" says
Peter, acting surprised and puzzled and looking
around as if seeking support from invisible companions. "How dare she say such a thing!" The crowing
of a rooster breaks in on Peter's performance.

Meanwhile, the high priest begins the inter-
rogation that is as fruitless as it is irreverent. Jesus
responds by quoting a passage from Scripture (Dn
7:13). By this time Peter is trying to distance himself from the portress, who keeps looking at him.
Every now and then he furtively glances in her direction. When at last he sees that the portress has
gone on about her business, he breathes a sigh of
relief.

During the night the temperature falls and fires
are started, around which the servants and the
guards gather to keep warm. Peter also moves closer
to the fire. All is quiet, but the disciple is being observed. One of the servants, a relative of Malchus,
whose ear Peter had cut off in the Garden of
Gethsemane, recognizes him. "Didn't I see you with
him in the Garden? Yes; I remember!" he said, rais-
ing his voice. "If Malchus were here he would also

remember! You are one of the followers of the man who was arrested."

Peter acts indignant. "I don't even know the man you're talking about," he insists. "Someone who looks like me must have been in the place you're talking about."

Peter prudently edges away from the group. But again he finds himself face to face with the young gatekeeper who had followed him and rejoined him. She keeps staring at him and then she bursts out in a loud voice: "Yes, I'm sure, you were also one of the followers of that man who was arrested!" At this point Peter begins to curse and swear that it is not true. He doesn't even know what the woman is talking about.

Jesus hears this at a distance and surely must be thinking that Peter's self-defense is somewhat exaggerated, to say the least! He is in fact going beyond bounds. Ah, men! And when Jesus hears the rooster crow for the second time, he begins to smile knowingly.

Peter also hears the rooster crow the second time, His heart is overwhelmed with sorrow and he begins to weep bitterly.

John and Peter Run to the Tomb

Here we have the story of the strange race of Peter and John to the empty tomb. The beloved disciple arrives first, but fear and deference prevent him from entering. He lets Peter go in first.

From the Gospel according to John (20:1-10):

On the first day of the week Mary Magdalen came to the tomb in the early morning while it was still dark, and she saw the stone, which had been taken away from the tomb. So she ran and came to Simon Peter and to the other disciple whom Jesus loved, and she said to them, "They've taken the Lord out of the tomb and we don't know where they've put him."

Peter and the other disciple went out and they went to the tomb. The two of them were running together, but the other disciple ran faster than Peter and came to the tomb first, and when he bent down he saw the linen cloths lying there, but he didn't go in. Simon Peter came, too, following him, and he went into the tomb and saw the linen cloths lying there, and the face covering, which had been on his head, wasn't lying with the linen cloths but was wrapped up separately in its own place. So then the other disciple, who had come first, went in, too, and he saw and believed, for they didn't yet understand the scripture that he had to rise from the dead. So the disciples went off home again.

This incident proclaims one of the greatest mysteries of the Christian faith: the resurrection of Christ, and it does so by describing the empty tomb. Unlike Matthew, John does not speak of the extraordinary events that preceded this episode, such as the earthquake; the angel, whose "appearance was like lightning and his clothing as white as snow," sent from heaven to move the heavy stone and announce to the women that Christ has risen; the guards paralyzed with fear (Mt 28:1-7). Neither does he report the announcement of the two men dressed in white: "Why are you looking for Him Who Lives among the dead? He isn't here — he's risen" (Lk 24:1-5). Nor does he mention the young man dressed in white, who startled Mary Magdalen and the women who were with her by announcing that Jesus had risen from the dead. On hearing this, "the women went out and fled the tomb, for trembling and amazement had seized them, and they said nothing to anyone because they were afraid" (Mk 16:1-8). John expresses himself succinctly, without mentioning the supernatural, except at the end of his account he says that the "other disciple... saw and believed" (Jn 20:9).

At the beginning of this passage we find the beloved apostle in the house with Peter and perhaps with others as well. Mary Magdalen arrives breath-less and exclaims: "They've taken the Lord out of the tomb and we don't know where they've put him!" There is a moment of consternation and then the two disciples leave and run to the tomb to see with their own eyes what has happened there.

The day is comfortably warm; wherever one looks, springtime is bursting out all over. The two disciples start running side by side but John, who is young and strong and a faster runner, arrives first at the tomb, while Peter, who is less vigorous, is still some distance behind. The younger disciple knows that he is the one best loved by Jesus, and he has stated this several times with satisfaction; but Peter has been named the head of the new Church by Christ. Perhaps because of this John found it a bit amusing to pass on ahead and leave Peter behind on the road. Jesus observes this from above and smiles.

When the beloved disciple arrives at the tomb, he bends down to peer inside. There is very little light inside but he notices the funeral wrappings lying on the ground. He does not enter, however. It is true that the Master had spoken about eternal life and the kingdom of heaven and had explained these things to his disciples, and in particular to the apostles, his loved ones. But for an ordinary human being a corpse is always a corpse. There is a certain fear of coming upon it. But if it is true that they have taken the body away and no one knows where it is?....

And what about the linen cloths lying on the ground? There are two possibilities: either the corpse has really been carried away or else it has shed the wrappings because it has really come back to life. John feels a cold sweat down his back. In either case he can't see that the situation will have a tranquil ending. Better to wait for Peter. After all, isn't he the one in charge? So although John arrives at the tomb first, he decides that it is better to let the older man enter and investigate the matter.

A few moments later Peter arrives, out of breath and very anxious to find out what has happened. He enters the tomb without delay. He sees "the linen cloths lying there, and the face covering, which had been on his head, wasn't lying with the linen cloths but was wrapped up separately in its own place" (Jn 20:7).

Therefore, he reasons, if the body had been taken away, the linen cloths and the face covering would not still be in the tomb. Much less would the face covering be folded up and lying in a place apart. Something much greater must have happened, something incomprehensible. In spite of the fact that they had been forewarned, in spite of the fact that they had lived for a long time with him for whom nothing is impossible, the resurrection of Christ is not easy to understand or to accept.

Complete silence reigns. Peter doesn't say a word, He doesn't summon the other disciple. He has other thoughts in his mind. John, meanwhile, comes to the conclusion that there is no reason to be afraid. He finally decides to enter the tomb also. He sees and he believes. Previously he had not understood the Scripture.

As for us, we are left with the unattainable desire to have heard the cries long ago of Mary Magdalen when she arrived at the house where the apostles were; to have joined Peter and John in their breathless race to the tomb; to have shared John's fear of entering the tomb and finally to attain with him the certitude of faith.

Perhaps Jesus smiled at John's narration of this event and especially at the touch of self-deprecation when he says: "So then the other disciple, who had come first, went in, too, and he saw and believed, for they didn't yet understand the scripture that he had to rise from the dead" (Jn 20:8-9).

The Gardener at the Tomb

Mary Magdalen mistakenly thinks that the risen Christ is the gardener of the cemetery. The disciples pay scant heed to the words of the women. The greatest miracle of Christ — his resurrection — has taken place, but practically no one knows about it as yet.

The most important thing for the moment is simply that the body of Jesus is no longer in the tomb. The question is whether it has been carried away.

When Peter and John arrive on the scene in order to investigate, at first they have an intuition and then they believe that the predicted resurrection has occurred. They then return home.

From the Gospel according to John (20:11-18):

Now Mary stood near the tomb, weeping outside. As she wept she looked into the tomb and saw two angels in white sitting where Jesus' body had been, one at the head and one at the feet. And they said to her, "Woman, why are you weeping?" She said to them, "They've taken my Lord and I don't know where they've put him!"

After she said this she turned around and saw Jesus standing there, yet she didn't realize that it was Jesus. Jesus said to her, "Woman, why are you weeping? Who are you looking for?" Thinking that it was the gardener she said to him, "Sir, if you removed him tell me where you put him, and I'll take him away." Jesus said to her, "Mary!" She turned and said to him, in Hebrew: "Rabboni!" which means "Teacher!"

Jesus said to her, "Don't touch me — I haven't yet ascended to the Father. But go to my brothers and tell them,

'I am ascending to my Father and your Father, And to my God and your God.'"

Mary Magdalen came and told the disciples, "I've seen the Lord!" and that he told her these things.

This is surely one of the most exciting, moving and sensitive passages in all the Gospels. The angels (who did not appear to Peter and John) and the risen Christ (who had not yet ascended to the Father), though denied to the sight of the two disciples, appear nevertheless to Mary Magdalen and the other women. The mistaken identity of Christ is immediately replaced by the woman's impulsive embrace of his feet. She just could not resist this manifestation of affection.

John's pen is so dynamic that at the distance of two thousand years it is able to report to us as if still physically present and it arouses in us the same emotion as it did in Mary Magdalen. And the text is so vivid and joyous that it makes us smile and in all probability it makes Jesus smile as well.

Mary Magdalen is speaking with the angels, but she probably doesn't recognize them as such. She speaks to them like a person in the throes of desperation. They have crucified the Master.

Mary Magdalen had remained in the vicinity of Calvary until the very end, but at a distance, together with Mary, the mother of James the younger and Joses, with Salome, and numerous others who had come out from Jerusalem (Mk 15:40). She did all she could to find out where they planned to lay the body afterwards. In fact, it is written that when the huge stone was rolled over the entrance to the tomb, "Mary Magdalen and the other Mary were there, sitting across from the sepulchre" (Mt 27:61; Mk 15:47).

At sunrise on the day after the Sabbath, Mary Magdalen hastens to the tomb with the perfumed oil to embalm the body of Jesus and she finds the stone rolled back and the tomb empty. She hastens to advise Peter and John and they in turn run to the tomb to find out for themselves what has happened. John reaches the tomb first; then Peter arrives. Perhaps Mary Magdalen is left standing at some distance. The two disciples enter the empty tomb, one after the other. They draw their own conclusions and return to the house. They don't say a word to Mary Magdalen. Obviously, at that moment Mary Magdalen has no influence on the behavior of the two disciples.

Actually, between the woman and the two

disciples (as between women in general and the male disciples) there is a certain amount of diffidence. Other witnesses in fact state that Mary Magdalen was not alone on that occasion; she was in the company of Joanna and Mary, the mother of James. And when they went together to tell the eleven and the other companions about the empty tomb, not only did they not believe it, but "it all seemed like nonsense to them" (Lk 24:11).

Likewise later, when Mary Magdalen returns to the house, Mark tells us that "when they heard that he was alive and had been seen by her they refused to believe" (Mk 16:11). The apostles and the other disciples simply cannot believe the testimony of Mary Magdalen and other witnesses who say that Christ has risen from the dead. This is just too incredible to be readily accepted. And to tell the truth, there are many others who can be put in the same category with doubting Thomas.

Returning to the Gospel according to John, when the two disciples left Mary Magdalen standing in front of the tomb weeping, her state of mind was not conducive to recognizing the two angels, however beautiful and luminous. At that moment perhaps their presence didn't make much of an impact. She was just hoping that someone could give her some information that would help her recover the body of her beloved Master, the Master who had liberated her from seven demons (Lk 8:2).

Consequently, preoccupied as she is, when

someone behind her, whom she does not recognize, asks her, "Woman, why are you weeping? Who are you looking for?" she thought she was being questioned by the gardener of the cemetery. Jesus, the living God, newly risen from the dead, is mistaken for the gardener! Not only that, but he is made the target of a slightly veiled accusation: "Sir, if you removed him, tell me where you put him, and I'll take him away."

In other words, it could be that you, the custodian of this cemetery, had every good reason for moving to another location the body of the person who is most dear to me. Why you did it doesn't matter. Just tell me where you've put it and, cost what it may, I'll go and carry it away without asking anyone's help.

Though he may have been smiling at the outset, Jesus now is deeply moved at the intense suffering of Mary Magdalen. As he had done many, many times before, he pronounces her name, as only he can pronounce it: "Mary!"

Mary's reaction is immediate; she turns to him, saying, "Rabboni!" Then she prostrates herself and embraces his feet. This is for her a moment filled with intense emotion. Jesus is deeply moved and he smiles down at Mary.

One of the many considerations inspired by this passage from the Gospel according to John is the following: Jesus came into this world through a woman, the Virgin Mary. And after his death and resurrection he manifested himself first of all to a woman: Mary Magdalen (Mk 16:9; Jn 20:11-18) or to several women (Mt 28:9). This is enough to make women smile and to make men think.

On the Road to Emmaus

On the road to Emmaus Cleopas and another disciple are joined by the risen Christ. They do not recognize the Master even when he speaks to them, and they treat him like a stranger who knows nothing about recent events.

From the Gospel according to Luke (24:13-35):

And, behold, two of them were travelling the same day to a village seven miles away from Jerusalem named Emmaus, talking to each other about all these events. And it happened while they were talking and discussing these things that Jesus himself approached and began to walk with them, but their eyes were kept from recognizing him. So he said to them, "What are these words you're exchanging with each other as you walk?"

They stopped gloomily, and in answer one named Cleopas said to him, "Are you the only person staying in Jerusalem who's unaware of what happened there in these days?" "What things?" he said. So they told him, "Those concerning Jesus of Nazareth, who was a prophet mighty in word and deed before God and all the people, how the chief priests and our rulers handed him over under sentence of death and had him crucified.

"We were hoping that he was the one who was coming to liberate Israel, but with all these things it's now the third day since this happened. Moreover, some women from among us have amazed us. They were at the tomb early in the morning and didn't find his body, and they came and said they'd even seen a vision of angels, who said he was alive. Some of those with us went off to the tomb, and they, too, found it just as the women said, but they didn't see him." He said to them, "How dense you are, and how slow of heart to believe all the prophets said! Didn't the Messiah have to suffer all these things and go into his glory?" And starting from Moses and all the prophets he interpreted for them what was in all the scriptures about himself.

They were approaching the village to which they were traveling, and when he made as if to travel further they urged him and said, "Stay with us, because it's near evening and the day has already come to a close." So he went in to stay with them. And it happened that when he reclined at table with them he took the bread and blessed it, broke it, and gave it to them. Then their eyes were opened and they recognized him, and he disappeared from them. And they said to each other, "Weren't our hearts burning within us while he spoke to us on the road, as he opened up the scriptures to us?" They got up and returned to Jerusalem that very hour, and they found the Eleven and those with them gathered together, saying, "The Lord has really risen and has been seen by Simon!" And they related what had happened on the road, and how they recognized him in the breaking of the bread.

Mark reports the same incident in a few words and without the details (Mk 16:12-13). This fact may seem rather strange, considering that Luke had consulted the Gospel according to Mark in order to write his own. But it is well to remember also that Luke, the Syrian doctor, had accompanied Paul on his missionary journeys and that Paul had had numerous contacts with the Eleven and with other disciples who had been eye-witnesses of many Gospel events. Consequently, he did not lack either the time or the occasions to gather more particulars that were necessary for writing his account. It is a fact that the meeting of Jesus with the two disciples on the road to Emmaus, as narrated by Luke, has stirred the conscience of millions of people throughout the centuries.

On that particular day the sun was shining and the sky was clear, as is usually the case in Palestine. The landscape is serene, the hills are a vibrant green, the road is practically deserted. Two men are walking along the road and talking about the dramatic events that have occurred in the last few days: the Master's condemnation to death, his crucifixion, the report that he has risen from the dead. This last item is still under discussion, since it was reported only by the women who had gone to the tomb to embalm his body. Engrossed as they are in their conversation, the two travellers do not notice that another pedestrian is overtaking them. And Jesus falls into step with them. In those days it was quite common for a traveller to catch up with others and join them on the journey.

The Master immediately recognizes the two disciples, but the same cannot be said about the disciples when they meet the Master. It could be that the body of Jesus has changed somewhat as a result of the resurrection. However, their failure to recognize the Master is more likely the result of their stubbornness and their lack of faith in the words of Scripture. Moreover, it is not insignificant that Cleopas is still convinced that Jesus should have liberated Israel.

Confronted with this situation, Jesus smiles to himself. He decides to speak to them; they will surely recognize him then. But they still take him for a stranger who is uninformed about events. "Are you the only person staying in Jerusalem who is unaware of what happened there in these days?" It's a dramatic moment but it is also rather amusing. At least it is so for Jesus, who tries again to make them recognize him. He exclaims: "How dense you are, and how slow of heart to believe all the prophets said!" He then explains to them the meaning of the Scriptures, which they should know well. Point by point he explains the prophecies: what is supposed to happen and what actually did happen.

But to no avail! The two disciples still do not realize that Jesus is with them. At least by this time they should start to have an inkling. They are aware of the report from the women who went to the tomb three days after the crucifixion. They know that the body of Christ was not in the place where they laid it. But they prefer to believe that the account given by the women was the result of a vision of angels or something worse. After all, the women were not believed by the Eleven either.

In the face of such stubbornness, Jesus has to smile at first, but then he is concerned. They arrive at the destination of the two disciples and Jesus gives the impression that he is going to continue his journey. But the day is about to end, and good manners dictate that one should offer overnight lodging to one's travelling companion. The roads are dangerous at night.

Jesus accepts their invitation and enters their house. They recognize him only at the blessing of the bread, which he breaks and gives to them. Then he disappears.

The two disciples will always regret that they missed out on the most unique opportunity of their lives. Jesus will smile many times as he recalls this missed opportunity and we smile with him when we read this passage in the Gospel according to Luke. But our smile fades quickly and is extinguished. We are prompted as if by instinct to identify with the two disciples on the road to Emmaus, and try as we may, we cannot rid ourselves of this identification. As a consequence we are confronted by two questions.

First of all, if we had been in their place, would we have recognized Jesus?

Second, if we were to come face to face with Jesus today on the street, at our work, while driving, how would we act? And is he not always at our side?

The challenge posed by this incident for countless generations of believers for two thousand years as they read the Gospel according to Luke is destined to be repeated in perpetuity.

Jesus is Mistaken for a Ghost

The risen Jesus appears in the midst of his
beloved disciples and is mistaken for a ghost.
He shows them his hands and feet, with the marks
of the crucifixion, but he is still not recognized.
Only after he has eaten a portion of broiled fish are
the disciples certain that he is really present.

From the Gospel according to Luke (24:36-43):

Now as they were speaking of these things
Jesus stood among them and said to them, "Peace
be with you!" But they were startled and terrified, thinking they were seeing a spirit. And he
said to them, "Why are you frightened, and why
are doubts arising in your hearts? Look at my
hands and my feet — it's me! Touch me and see,
because a spirit doesn't have flesh and bones, as
you see I do! And as he said this he showed them
his hands and feet. But since they were still incredulous and wondering for joy, he said to
them, "Do you have anything to eat here?" So
they gave him a piece of broiled fish and he took
it and ate it in front of them.

Matthew relates that after the resurrection
Jesus appears to the Eleven in Galilee, on a moun-

tain to which he had directed them. It is like keeping an appointment. And he says only that some were doubtful (Mt 28:16-17). Nothing more. According to Mark, the appearance of Jesus is accompanied by a reprimand for incredulity and hardness of heart for not having believed in the news of his resurrection, as reported by those who had seen him (Mk 16:14).

John tells us that Jesus comes before the apostles and greets them with a marvelous salutation: "Peace be with you!" Only after that does he show them his hands and side so that they will recognize him (Jn 20:19-23). But let's return to Luke.

Early in the evening of the day after the Sabbath, the Eleven, together with some other disciples, are gathered together in a house with the doors securely closed for fear of the Jews. They are sad and confused, but with hope in their hearts. It is the hour of twilight and the rooms are getting dark. The blazing sunset is ignored. In the previous hours the news about the resurrection has been circulated, but as yet there is no verification.

The appearance of Jesus to Mary Magdalen and the other women, the investigation of the empty tomb by Peter and John, and the appearance to Peter himself should have dispelled all doubt. But there still remains an air of mystery. Of course, a certain hesitation is to be expected. After all, we are faced with a truly extraordinary event, the most extraordinary in all human history.

More than once the Master had raised the dead: the son of the widow of Nain (Lk 7:11-17), the daughter of Jairus (Mt 9:18-26; Mk 5:22-43; Lk 8:41-56), and his friend Lazarus (Jn 11:1-44), but until now no one in the entire history of the world has ever risen by his own power. We can imagine the conversation of the disciples gathered together in that house and the many reasons Jesus has to smile.

As dusk is gathering at the close of that day, therefore, and with the doors and windows of the house in which the apostles and disciples are gathered tightly secured, behold, Jesus presents himself in person! They are overwhelmed with astonishment and they shiver with fear. They think that they are seeing an apparition. The same thing had happened before when they saw Jesus walking on the water to join his disciples who were in the boat (Mt 14:26; Mk 6:49). And from a human point of view, as we have already said, they have good reason to be frightened again this time. And Jesus also this time has reason to smile.

But the Master is good, infinitely good. He tries to convince them that it is really himself by showing them the wounds of the crucifixion. Their astonishment and fear do not vanish immediately, but at the same time their joy reaches such a pitch that they are completely beside themselves.

At this point Jesus asks them for something to eat. They give him a piece of broiled fish and he eats it. A ghost would not do that, the disciples say to themselves. Of course not!

This Gospel passage also makes us smile, but it vanishes as soon as we consider once more the possibility of suddenly seeing Jesus appear before us in person.

Surely their joy is immense, but their fear is equally great. Then little by little they return to reality. They have realized their hope of achieving certitude concerning him and the true meaning of our existence. It is a clear and definitive victory over feelings of remorse and regret in exchange for a life spent in proclaiming the future glory of the world.

Thomas, Thomas!

On the evening of the third day after the death of Jesus,
he is seen by his disciples, who are gathered together
because of fear of the Jews, but one of the disciples,
Thomas, called the Twin, is absent. When, in the midst
of joy and excitement, he is told of the appearance of the
Master, he replies that he will believe what they
tell him only if he sees the mark of the nails in
Jesus' hands and can put his hand into his side.
With such an attitude Thomas merits the title of the most
incredulous man in the whole world and of all times.

From the Gospel according to John (20:19-29):

When it was evening on that first day of the
week, and the doors had been locked where the
disciples were for fear of the Jews, Jesus came and
stood in their midst and said to them, "Peace be
with you!" And after saying this he showed them
his hands and side, So the disciples rejoiced to
see the Lord. He said to them again, "Peace be
with you! As the Father has sent me, I, too, send
you." And after saying this he breathed on them
and said, "Receive the Holy Spirit!

Whoever's sins you forgive,
    they've already been forgiven,
Whoever's you retain,
    they've already been retained."

Now Thomas, one of the Twelve, called the Twin, wasn't with them when Jesus came. So the other disciples told him, "We've seen the Lord!" But he told them, "Unless I see the mark of the nails in his hands and put my finger into the mark of the nail and put my hand into his side, I won't believe!"

And a week later his disciples were once again inside, and Thomas was with them. Although the doors had been locked, Jesus came and stood in their midst and said, "Peace be with you!"

Then he said to Thomas,

"Bring your finger here
    and look at my hands,
And bring your hand
    and put it in my side,
And be not unbelieving,
    but believing!"

Thomas answered and said to him, "My Lord and my God!" Jesus said to him,

"You've believed because you've seen me;
Blessed are they who haven't seen
    yet have believed!"

Matthew reports that the risen Jesus appeared to the disciples on a mountain in Galilee and, as soon as they saw him, they prostrated themselves, although some of them doubted that it was really the Master (Mt 28:16-17). Mark relates the same incident but he says that Jesus appeared while the disciples were at table and he reprimanded them for their unbelief (Mk 16:14). According to Luke, when Jesus stood among them the disciples thought they were seeing a ghost, and they were terrified. It took a bit of talking and a showing of his wounds to convince them that they were not seeing an apparition. In the end, Jesus had to eat a piece of broiled fish in order to prove that it was really himself in flesh and bone.

There are plenty of reasons to make one smile. Think of it! Jesus, God and man, having to do these things to prove his identity!

John is the only one of the Evangelists to give us the name of the most incredulous apostle, and the most obstinate in his doubt. It is Thomas, known as the Twin. He even gives his nickname! So there can be no mistake.

He was not present the first time that Jesus appeared to the disciples. But the other disciples told him that Jesus had come to them. Most likely they also told Thomas about the appearance of Jesus to Mary Magdalen and the other women at the tomb, the incident involving Cleopas and his companion on the road to Emmaus, as well as the investigation of Peter and John at the sepulcher. Besides, Thomas himself should have been well aware that the Scriptures, the prophets and Jesus himself had spoken of the coming, the death and the resurrection of the Messiah.

But all that is not enough. Not at all. Thomas insists that he will not believe in the resurrection of the Master "unless I see the mark of the nails in his hands and put my finger into the mark of the nail and put my hand into his side" (Jn 20:25). He is really hard-headed! There's nothing more to say.

Thus, eight days later Jesus returns to his disciples. This time Thomas, the Twin, is with them. Jesus greets them all and then immediately turns to that champion of doubters. "Look at me," says Jesus; "touch my hands that were wounded by the nails and my side that was pierced by the soldier's lance." At this point Thomas falls to his knees: "My Lord and my God!" Jesus warns the entire human race: "Blessed are they who haven't seen, yet have believed!"

One Must Know How to Fish

Jesus appears again to some of the disciples
on the shore of the Sea of Tiberias, but once more they
do not recognize him. But after a miraculous
catch of fish, they realize that they are in the
presence of Jesus. Naked in the boat, Peter quickly
covers himself and then jumps into the water
in order to join the Master on the shore.

From the Gospel according to John (21:1-14):

After these things Jesus again showed himself to the disciples at the Sea of Tiberias. Now he appeared in this way: Simon Peter and Thomas, who was called the Twin, and Nathanael, who was from Cana in Galilee, and the sons of Zebedee and two others of his disciples were together. Simon Peter said to them, "I'm going fishing." They said to him, "We're going with you, too." They went out and got in the boat and that night they caught nothing.

Now as day was breaking Jesus stood there on the shore, but the disciples didn't know that it was Jesus. So Jesus said to them, "Children, do you have any fish?" They answered him, "No." Then he said to them, "Cast the net to the right side of the boat and you'll find some." So they cast it, and now they were unable to draw it in because of the number of fish.

So the disciple Jesus loved said to Peter, "It's the Lord!" Simon Peter, when he heard that it was the Lord, put on his outer garment — he was stripped — and threw himself into the sea. Then the other disciples came with the boat — they weren't far from land, about a hundred yards away — dragging the net of fish.

So as they were coming up onto land they saw a charcoal fire started and a fish laid on it and bread. Jesus said to them, "Bring some of the fish you caught just now." Simon Peter went aboard and dragged the net to land, full of large fish — a hundred and fifty-three — yet, even though there were so many, the net wasn't split. Jesus said to them, "Come eat breakfast!" Now none of the disciples dared to ask him, "Who are you?" because they knew it was the Lord. Jesus came and took the bread and gave it to them, and likewise the fish. This was already the third time Jesus had appeared to the disciples after rising from the dead.

Everything has been accomplished. The earthly life of Jesus after the resurrection is coming to an end. Seven of his disciples are together on this occasion. They know that from now on their life will be different. It is hard for them really to believe that the Master has risen and is travelling around Galilee; it is difficult to believe that they have been entrusted with a mission that will perdure throughout the centuries and even to the end of the world. They will experience the descent of the Holy Spirit to strengthen them in the faith and increase their capability. No one could possibly have imagined at that time that in the future the entire human race will have a well-defined relationship with those seven.

So Simon Peter, James and John, Thomas, Nathanael and two others are together. The first ones are expert fishermen. They were called by Jesus when they had returned from fishing and were in the boat repairing their nets. It is evident that their commitment is still strong.

Nathanael is an intellectual and like all intellectuals he thinks that everything is possible and easy for him, even fishing. The events of the preceding days have been very trying and difficult to understand. A good ride on the sea will be helpful for all of them. It is Peter who suggests it. It's a quiet evening and they are on the shore, in the vicinity of the Seven Fountains. The sight of the calm waters is inviting. Only a few words are needed: "I'm going fishing." The others immediately respond with joy or perhaps with a sense of liberation.

They wade into the water, climb into the boat, shove off and let down their nets. They speak little. Jesus is not with them but he knows all their thoughts.

The night passes, but the nets are still empty. Those expert fishermen do not make much of that.

They have put to sea in order to relax for a time, but their habitual thoughts and concerns are still with them.

At dawn Jesus is present on the shore. He watches them return. When they are close enough, he asks the men in the boat if they have anything to eat. It is a nice way to get their attention. Perhaps they have heard this same question numerous times in the past few years. But the disciples do not recognize Jesus, even though this is the third time that he has appeared to them. They are somewhat disappointed and they answer the Master's question with a simple "No."

"Cast the net to the right side of the boat," says the as yet unknown man on the shore. Halfheartedly they comply. What's there to lose?

But... What's happening? The boat is listing to the right side. The net is filled to overflowing with fish. John is the first one to catch on. "It's the Lord!" he says to Simon Peter, fired with enthusiasm for that magnificent catch of fish such as he has not seen for a long time. The rest of the disciples now realize that it couldn't be anyone else but him. Peter is beside himself with joy.

Jesus is also happy. He smiles when he sees that the head of his Church suddenly realizes that he is naked and immediately wraps his outer garments around his waist. Peter then jumps into the water in order to be the first one to join him. Everyone in the boat is smiling. He who is on the shore also smiles when he sees that disciple with the beard swimming toward him as if he were trying to break a speed record, as if waving him a greeting with every powerful stroke.

After swimming for approximately a hundred yards, Simon Peter reaches the shore and he doesn't know whether to throw himself at the feet of Jesus or embrace him. The joy is intense for all of them. The other six disciples drag the boat on shore with the net still hanging over the side. As soon as they approach Jesus and Peter, they see a fish cooking over a charcoal fire, and some bread. Jesus has prepared it for them. He asks for some more fish, so Peter goes down to the boat and pulls the net on shore. There are one hundred and fifty-three large fish in the net.

Jesus invites them all to eat breakfast. Some of the disciples still hesitate to ask him who he is. Of course, they do know that they are in the presence of Jesus, but there is still a touch of incredulity remaining. So Jesus, smiling, puts them at ease and gives them bread and fish to eat.